Teaching Study Skills and Strategies to Students with Learning Disabilities, Attention Deficit Disorders, or Special Needs

Teaching Study Skills and Strategies to Students with Learning Disabilities, Attention Deficit Disorders, or Special Needs

Second Edition

STEPHEN S. STRICHART
Florida International University

CHARLES T. MANGRUM II
University of Miami–Coral Gables

PATRICIA IANNUZZI
Florida International University

Allyn and Bacon
Boston   London   Toronto   Sydney   Tokyo   Singapore

Series editor: Ray Short
Series editorial assistant: Karin Huang
Marketing manager: Kathy Hunter
Manufacturing buyer: Suzanne Lareau

Library of Congress Cataloging-in-Publication Data

Strichart, Stephen S.
   Teaching study skills and strategies to students with learning
 disabilities, attention deficit disorders, or special needs /
 Stephen S. Strichart, Charles T. Mangrum II, Patricia Iannuzzi.—
 2nd ed.
     p.   cm.
   Rev. ed. of: Teaching study strategies to students with learning
 disabilities. c1993.
   Includes bibliographical references.
   ISBN 0-205-27469-2
   1. Learning disabled children—Education (Elementary)—United
 States. 2. Learning disabled teenagers—Education (Secondary)-
 -United States. 3. Study skills—United States. 4. Special
 education—United States. I. Mangrum, Charles T. II. Iannuzzi,
 Patricia. III. Strichart, Stephen S. Teaching study strategies to
 students with learning disabilities. IV. Title.
 LC4704.73.S77 1998
 371.91′4—dc21
                                                                         97-52619
                                                                            CIP

Printed in the United States of America
10 9 8 7 6   02 01 00

Contents

CHAPTER SIX
Using the Internet   **95**

CHAPTER SEVEN
Using Reference Sources   **117**

Introduction

HOW THIS BOOK WILL HELP

This book provides opportunities for active learning by students in grades 4 through 12 with learning disabilities (LD), attention deficit disorders (ADD), or special needs. The activities will help these students master study skills and strategies important for success in many subject areas. Teaching students to use study skills and strategies effectively is an important step in transforming dependent learners into independent learners. The activities are designed to help students become independent learners in an increasingly technology-based learning environment.

Accompanying this book is a trial version of a computer assessment titled "Study Skills and Strategies Assessment—Special Edition" (3S-SE). 3S-SE assesses students' use of the study skills and strategies taught in this book. The free trial disk, available in Windows only, can be administered to five students. A disk with an unlimited number of administrations may then be purchased in either Windows or Macintosh versions. The order form is found on page 235.

FEATURES OF THIS BOOK

This book incorporates features designed to meet the needs of students with LD, ADD, or special needs. These features include:

1. Coverage of the important study skills and strategies
2. Opportunities for practice and application
3. Mastery Assessments for each chapter
4. Brief and easily understood student directions
5. Controlled amount of material on a page
6. Bold type and italics
7. Controlled readability
8. Controlled vocabulary
9. Focus on strategies
10. Incorporation of subject-area information

STUDY STRATEGIES TAUGHT IN THIS BOOK

The study skills and strategies taught in this book are those most important for success by students in grades 4–12 with LD, ADD, or special needs. The study skills and strategies are presented in the following eleven chapters:

Chapter One
Strategies for Remembering Information

Learning something is of little value if what is learned cannot be recalled whenever necessary. In this chapter, students are taught strategies they can use to retain the important information and ideas they learn from their teachers and textual materials.

Chapter Two
Reading and Taking Notes from Textbooks

Much of the information students must learn in school is contained in their textbooks. Students must be taught how to obtain information from their textbooks effectively and efficiently. To do so, students must have a textbook reading and notetaking strategy. In this chapter, students are taught to use a textbook reading and notetaking strategy called SQRW.

Chapter Three
Solving Math Word Problems

Having a strategy helps students solve math word problems. In this chapter, students are taught to use a math word problem-solving strategy called SQRQCQ. They then are taught to apply the strategy to different types of math word problems.

Chapter Four
Taking Class Notes

Students must write in their notes the important information presented by their teachers. In this chapter, students are taught a strategy for taking class notes.

Chapter Five
Using the Library

Students must be taught to make appropriate use of the many print and electronic resources found in libraries. In this chapter, students are taught to use online catalogs and databases to find and evaluate information.

Chapter Six
Using the Internet

The Internet is a popular tool for locating information. In this chapter, students are taught about using e-mail and searching the World Wide Web. Students are also taught strategies to evaluate the information they find on the Internet.

Chapter Seven
Using Reference Sources

Students must be made aware of the many reference sources they can use to achieve success in school. In this chapter, students are taught strategies for using both print and electronic forms of these reference sources: dictionary, encyclopedia, thesaurus, almanac, and atlas.

Chapter Eight
Interpreting Graphic Aids

Students must be taught how to interpret maps, graphs, diagrams, tables, and charts to increase their understanding of information found in textual materials. In this chapter, students are taught strategies for interpreting these graphic aids.

Chapter Nine
Writing a Research Paper

Students must be able to do library research and write a research paper. They must be taught to obtain, document, and organize print and electronic information and present it in a clear, written form. In this chapter, students are taught a strategic series of steps to follow when writing a research paper.

Chapter Ten
Preparing for and Taking Tests

Students must demonstrate mastery of information by taking tests given in different formats. In this chapter, students are taught a five-day strategy for preparing for tests. They are also taught how to do well on the following types of tests: multiple choice, true/false, matching, completion, and essay.

Chapter Eleven
Making Good Use of Study Time and Space

Students must make effective use of their time to complete school assignments and prepare adequately for tests. Students also need good study habits to get good grades. They must also have a good place to study. In this chapter, students are taught strategies for scheduling their time, evaluating and improving their study habits, and organizing their study space.

HOW THIS BOOK IS ORGANIZED

Each chapter is organized as follows:

1. Objectives
2. Titles of Reproducible Activities
3. Using the Reproducible Activities
4. Reproducible Activities
5. Mastery Assessment
6. Answer Key

HOW TO USE THIS BOOK

1. Use your judgment and/or the results from 3S-SE to select the chapters most appropriate for your students.
2. Duplicate the reproducible activities you wish to use.
3. Use the suggestions in Using the Reproducible Activities and your own ideas to provide instruction.
4. Have students complete the Mastery Assessment at any point you feel students have learned the study skills and strategies presented in a chapter. Plan further instruction accordingly.

TEACHING NOTES

Here are some things to do when using this book:

1. Go beyond the reproducibles to provide your students with additional practice in the use of the strategies. It is additional practice with materials that are directly related to classroom objectives that will enable students to achieve greater success in school.
2. Have the students use a study strategy under your supervision until they have mastered it. Mastery of a strategy means that students are able to recall it as rapidly as they can recall their own names or phone numbers. Mastery also means the ability to apply the strategy automatically to school tasks. Students have achieved mastery when they can automatically recall and apply a strategy. Until they have achieved this automaticity, there is no mastery.
3. Share the strategies with colleagues who also teach your students, and encourage your colleagues to have the students use the strategies in their classes as well. This will help to ensure that students generalize and maintain their use of the strategies.
4. Although the various study strategies are presented individually in this book, in reality students will need to use a combination of

strategies to complete most assignments. For example, students studying for a test should use strategies for remembering information, reading textbooks, and managing time, in addition to test-taking strategies. Use every opportunity to demonstrate or explain to your students how to combine the use of the various strategies presented in this book.

5. Motivate your students to want to use the study strategies taught in this book. We recommend you use the PARS motivation strategy. This strategy has four components: Purpose, Attitude, Results, Success.

   - *Purpose.* Students are more likely to want to learn a study strategy when they understand how the strategy can help them succeed in school. Be sure to explain how its use can help them acquire more information and get better grades in your class and in their other classes.
   - *Attitude.* Your attitude is infectious. If you are enthusiastic about a study strategy, your enthusiasm will transfer to your students, who are then likely to model your positive attitude toward the use of the strategy.
   - *Results.* It is important to give students feedback on how well they are applying a strategy. The feedback needs to be very specific so that students understand what they did correctly and what they did wrong. Students need specific feedback in order to know what to do to improve their use of each strategy.
   - *Success.* It is important that students experience success in the application of a strategy. Nothing elicits recurrent behavior as well as success.

6. Have students work cooperatively in pairs or small groups to practice applying the strategies to class assignments. Students can take turns demonstrating how a strategy is used or providing feedback on the effectiveness of its use.

Acknowledgments

We express our appreciation to our colleagues at the University of Miami and Florida International University who graciously gave their time to review the activities in this book. Their reactions and recommendations were of great assistance to us. We also wish to acknowledge our university students, many of whom are teachers of students with LD, ADD, or special needs. Feedback from their use of the activities in their mainstreamed, inclusive, and special-education classrooms was extremely helpful to us.

About the Authors

Stephen S. Strichart is professor of special education and learning disabilities at Florida International University, Miami, Florida. He graduated from City College of New York and taught children with various types of disabilities before entering graduate school. Dr. Strichart earned a Ph.D. from Yeshiva University in 1972. Since 1975 he has been on the faculty at Florida International University, where he trains teachers and psychologists to work with exceptional students. Dr. Strichart is the author of many books and articles on topics related to special education and study skills.

Charles T. Mangrum II is professor of special education and reading at the University of Miami, Coral Gables, Florida. He graduated from Northern Michigan University and taught elementary and secondary school before entering graduate school. He earned a Ed.D. from Indiana University in 1968. Since 1968 he has been on the faculty at the University of Miami, where he trains teachers who teach students with reading and learning disabilities. Dr. Mangrum is the author of many books, instructional programs, and articles on topics related to reading and study skills.

Patricia Iannuzzi is University Librarian and Head of the Reference Department at Florida International University Libraries. She graduated from Yale University and earned an M.S. in Library and Information Science at Simmons College in 1980. Ms. Iannuzzi has worked in libraries at Tufts University, Yale University, and the University of California at Berkeley. Since 1990 she has been on the library faculty at Florida International University, where she manages reference services, develops information literacy curricula, and teaches information literacy skills in subjects across the curriculum.

CHAPTER ONE

Strategies for Remembering Information

OBJECTIVES

1. Teach students to use a variety of strategies for remembering information.
2. Prompt students to reflect on their use of the various strategies.

TITLES OF REPRODUCIBLE ACTIVITIES

USING THE REPRODUCIBLE ACTIVITIES

After you have distributed a reproducible activity, here are suggestions for its use. Define any terms and clarify any concepts students do not know. Feel free to add further information, illustrations, or examples. Wherever possible, relate the activity to actual subject area assignments.

1-1 Thinking about How You Remember Information

Discuss the importance of remembering information. Have students write a statement describing what they do to remember information. Have students read about the strategies for remembering information they will learn to use in this chapter. Then have students complete the activity. Examine the strategies students identify as those about which they need to learn more. Use this information to guide you as you select the reproducible activities most appropriate to use with your students.

1-2 Repetition Strategy

Repetition involves reading, writing, and reciting information a number of times to remember it. For example, repetition is a common strategy used by students to remember a list of names and dates for a history test.

Introduce the repetition strategy. Have students complete the activity. Finally, have students reflect and write a statement that tells when they would use the repetition strategy.

1-3 Mind Picture Strategy

Mind pictures are mental images or pictures created in the mind and later used to recall information. The mental images serve as a place to collect and hold together facts to be remembered. By including names, dates, and places in their pictures, students can remember a substantial collection of information. Mind picture is a useful strategy for remembering such things as a series of events in history or the geographical features associated with a region.

Introduce the mind picture strategy. Have students place the letter P (for *picture*) in front of sets of information that are appropriately remembered using the mind picture strategy. Have students complete the activity. Finally, have students reflect and write a statement that tells when they would use the mind picture strategy.

1-4 Categorization Strategy

Categorization is a good way to remember things that go together. For example, a list of ten items is easier to remember if the items can be categorized into groups of items that go together.

Use the first part of the activity to demonstrate to students how categorization helps them remember more information. Then introduce the categorization strategy. Finally, have students reflect and write a statement that tells when they would use the categorization strategy.

1-5 Rhyme Strategy

Rhyme is the use of verse to remember information. Use familiar rhymes such as the following to demonstrate to students how rhyme is used to remember information.

> In fourteen hundred ninety-two
> Columbus sailed the ocean blue.
>
> Thirty days has September,
> April, June, and November.

Use the first part of the activity to demonstrate to students how rhyme can be used to remember information. Then introduce the rhyme strategy. Finally, have students reflect and write a statement that tells when they would use the rhyme strategy.

1-6 Abbreviation Strategy: Information in a Certain Order

Abbreviations are formed using the first letter of each word to be remembered. Abbreviations cannot be pronounced. Sometimes abbreviations have to be formed in a certain order to correspond to the order in which information must be remembered.

Use the first part of the activity to introduce students to abbreviation as a strategy for remembering information in a certain order. Have students write abbreviations. Review the abbreviation strategy. Finally, have students reflect and write a statement that tells when they would use the abbreviation strategy for information in a certain order.

1-7 Abbreviation Strategy: Information in Any Order

Sometimes abbreviations are formed for words that may be remembered in any order. In this case, students should be encouraged to arrange the letters in whatever order is easiest for them to remember.

Use the first part of the activity to introduce students to abbreviation as a strategy for remembering information in any order. Have students write abbreviations. Review the abbreviation strategy. Finally, have students reflect and write a statement that tells when they would use the abbreviation strategy for information in any order.

1-8 Acronym Strategy

Like abbreviations, acronyms are formed using the first letter of each word to be remembered. The letters are arranged to form a pronounceable "word." The acronym may be either a real word or a nonsense word. When an acronym cannot be formed, tell students to form an abbreviation instead.

Use the activity to demonstrate how acronyms can be either real or nonsense words. Have students form real and nonsense word acronyms. Review the acronym strategy. Finally, have students reflect and write a statement that tells when they would use the acronym strategy.

1-9 Acronymic Sentence Strategy

When using this remembering technique, students create sentences made up of words that begin with the initial letter of each of the items to be remembered. A common example used to remember the order of the planets in our solar system is this acronymic sentence: *My* (Mercury) *very* (Venus) *earthy* (Earth) *mother* (Mars) *just* (Jupiter) *served* (Saturn) *us* (Uranus) *nine* (Neptune) *pizzas* (Pluto). Tell students that acronymic sentences are useful to remember information for which it is difficult to form an acronym or for which an abbreviation would be too long to be remembered.

Use the introduction to provide students with an example of an acronymic sentence. Review the acronymic sentence strategy. Have students write acronymic sentences for the sets of information provided. Finally, have students reflect and write a statement that tells when they would use the acronym strategy.

1-10 Graphic Organizer Strategy

Graphic organizers are useful to remember information that is organized by topic, subtopics, and details. A graphic organizer is a visual representation of the information to be remembered.

Use the first activity to introduce and demonstrate the use of a graphic organizer. Review the graphic organizer strategy. Have students create a graphic organizer using the information provided. Finally, have students reflect and write a statement that tells when they would use the graphic organizer strategy.

1-11 Chapter One Mastery Assessment

Have students complete this assessment at any point you believe they have learned to use the remembering strategies presented in this chapter. Review the results of the assessment with students. Provide additional instruction as needed.

Think about the strategies you use to remember information for classes, tests, or in your day-to-day activities. Write a statement that tells about these strategies.

Here are remembering strategies that are taught in this chapter. Read about each. Place a check (✔) in front of each strategy that you included in the statement you wrote.

Repetition is a strategy in which you read, write, and recite information.

Mind Picture is a strategy in which you form one or more pictures in your mind.

Categorization is a strategy in which you place information to be remembered into categories.

Rhyme is a strategy in which you create lines of verse.

Abbreviation is a strategy in which you use the first letter of words to form an abbreviation.

Acronym is a strategy in which you use the first letter of words to form a new word.

Acronymic Sentence is a strategy in which you use the first letter of words to create a sentence.

Graphic Organizer is a strategy in which you show how facts are related or organized.

Write the names of the strategies about which you need to learn more.

When you read, write, and recite information a number of times to remember it, you are using repetition. Repetition is a good strategy to use when you must remember information such as names, dates, locations, and other such facts.

Here is how to use the repetition strategy:

1. Read silently the information to be remembered.
2. Write the information.
3. With your eyes closed, recite aloud the information you wrote.
4. Repeat steps 1–3 three times.
5. After 15 minutes, repeat step 3. If you do not remember the information, repeat steps 1–4.

Use the repetition strategy to remember the following information. Then answer the questions that follow.

Marco Polo explored Asia and travelled to China in the late 1200s. Christopher Columbus discovered America in 1492. Ferdinand Magellan sailed around the world in the early 1500s.

1. Were you able to remember the information after 15 minutes?

2. What type of information would you try to remember using the repetition strategy?

Another way to remember information is by forming one or more pictures in your mind. Forming pictures is a good way to remember the events in a story, things that occur in an order, and other information that is easily pictured in your mind.

Here is how to use the mind picture strategy:

1. Write or say aloud the information you need to remember.
2. As you write or say the information, form a picture of it in your mind. Try to place all the information in one picture. If you cannot, form a second or more pictures as needed.
3. With your eyes closed, look at the picture(s) in your mind. Say aloud the information you see.
4. Open your eyes and write the information.

Look at each of the following. Place the letter **P** in front of each that would be easy for you to remember by making a picture in your mind.

_____ **1.** The years 1914, 1940, 1950, 1970

_____ **2.** Major wars: World War I, World War II, Korean War, Vietnam War

_____ **3.** What you ate for your last meal

_____ **4.** The most interesting thing you did yesterday

_____ **5.** The events that took place in the last story you read

_____ **6.** Something you saw on TV

_____ **7.** The floats or bands that appeared in a parade

_____ **8.** The names of the last five presidents of the United States

Answer the following:

9. Would repetition be a good way to remember the information for which you did not write **P**? _____ Why?

10. What types of information are best remembered using the mind pictures strategy?

Categorization is another way to remember information. It is a good way to remember things that go together in some way.

Read the following set of items.

pencil	paper	magazine	pen	book
chalk	chalkboard	poem	cardboard	newspaper

1. Cover the set of items. Write all the items you can remember here.

2. Uncover the set of items. How many did you remember? Write the number here.

3. Read the set of items again. After you read an item, write it under one of the following category headings:

   Things to Write with   Things to Write on   Things to Read

4. Cover the category headings and items. Recall the three categories. Then write the items you remember from each category here.

5. Uncover the items. How many did you remember? Write the numbers here.

6. Did you remember more items by using categorization? _____ Why?

Here is how to use the categorization strategy:

   1. Write the information you need to remember.
   2. Look for information that goes together to form a category.
   3. Write the name of the first category. Then write the information that goes into that category.
   4. Repeat for each remaining category.

---

7. What type of information would you try to remember using the categorization strategy?

Another way to remember information is to form a rhyme. Usually in a rhyme, the words at the end of lines sound alike. Rhyme is a good strategy to use when the information you want to remember has words that sound alike.

Here is a rhyme with one set of words that sound alike:

> My friend's name is Harry.
> His sister's name is Mary.
> They both are going to a party held by Larry
> who lives at Terry Avenue.

1. What names was the person who made this rhyme trying to remember?

2. Who is having the party?

3. At what address?

Sometimes a rhyme has more than one set of words that sound alike:

> My friend's name is Harry.
> His sister's name is Mary.
> We are going to their party.
> And we don't want to be tardy.

4. Where are we going?

5. What do we *not* want to be?

You can also build a rhyme using a number word:

> Christopher Columbus was not a tailor
> What he was was a good old sailor
> He sailed across the ocean blue
> and discovered America in 1492.

6. What was Columbus?

7. What did he discover?

8. When?

Here is how to use the rhyme strategy:

1. Write the information you need to remember.
2. Underline the words that rhyme.
3. Write a line that ends with one of the words you underlined.
4. Write another line that ends with a word that rhymes with the word you underlined.
5. Repeat steps 3 and 4 for as many lines as you wish to write.

---

9. What type of information would you try to remember using the rhyme strategy?

Abbreviation is a good strategy to use when you want to remember a number of words. An abbreviation is formed using the first letter of each word to be remembered. An abbreviation cannot be pronounced.

Sometimes words have to be remembered in a certain order. For example, to remember three states—California, Pennsylvania, and Delaware—in order of population, you would use the abbreviation CPD.

Each of the following must be remembered in the order shown. Write an abbreviation for each.

1. Money in increasing order of value:

   penny, nickel, dime, quarter, dollar

2. Planets in order from outer space to the sun:

   Pluto, Neptune, Saturn, Jupiter, Mars

3. Students in order of height:

   Juan, Steve, Nu, Bob, Nell

4. Army officers in order of rank:

   lieutenant, captain, major, colonel, general

5. Highest percentage of population over age 65:

   Sweden, Germany, Italy, France

Here is how to use the abbreviation strategy when you want to remember information in a certain order:

1. Write the information you need to remember.
2. Circle the words that will help you remember the information.
3. Arrange the words you circled in the order they must be remembered.
4. Underline the first letter of each word you circled.
5. Write the underlined letters to form the abbreviation.

---

6. What type of information would you try to remember using the abbreviation strategy?

Sometimes the words to be remembered can be remembered in any order. Suppose you had to remember the colors purple, brown, and green in any order. Any of these abbreviations will work: *pbg, pgb, bpg, bgp, gpb, gbp.*

Each of the following may be remembered in any order. Write the abbreviation that would be easiest for you to remember:

1. nose, lungs, heart, kidneys

2. turkey, whale, goose, lion, seal

3. fins, scales, gills

4. Canada, Spain, Germany, France

5. broom, brush, pail, mop

Here is how to use the abbreviation strategy when you want to remember information in any order:

1. Write the information you need to remember.
2. Circle the words that will help you remember the information.
3. Underline the first letter of each word you circled.
4. Write the underlined letters in the order that is easiest for you to remember.

---

6. What type of information would you try to remember using the abbreviation strategy?

Acronym is another strategy for remembering a number of words. An acronym is a word formed from the first letter of each word to be remembered. The letters are arranged to form a word that can be pronounced.

An acronym may be a real word, as in these examples:

CALF	California, Arizona, Louisiana, Florida
tame	tiger, antelope, monkey, elephant

Write a real-word acronym for each of the following:

1. *States*: Delaware, Indiana, Nevada, Michigan

2. *Birds*: finch, owl, lark, wren

3. *Fruits and vegetables*: apple, tomato, lettuce, endive

An acronym may be a pronounceable nonsense word, as in these examples:

LEAT	Lincoln, Eisenhower, Adams, Truman
grib	green, red, indigo, blue

Write a pronounceable nonsense-word acronym for each of the following:

4. *American cities*: Chicago, Raleigh, Tacoma, Oakland

5. *Trees*: pine, oak, redwood, birch

6. *Fish*: bass, carp, salmon, eel

Here is how to use the acronym strategy:

1. Write the information you need to remember.
2. Circle the words that will help you remember the information.
3. Underline the first letter of each word you circled.
4. Arrange the underlined letters to write an acronym.

---

7. What type of information would you try to remember using the acronym strategy?

Acronymic sentences also can be used to remember information. An acronymic sentence is created from words whose first letter helps you remember information. For example, the following acronymic sentence was created to remember that **M**innesota, **W**isconsin, **I**llinois, **I**ndiana, **O**hio, and **M**ichigan all have a port on one of the Great Lakes:

Indians **w**ere **m**ining **o**re **i**n **M**innesota.

> Here is how to use the acronymic sentence strategy:
>
> 1. Write the information you need to remember.
> 2. Circle the words that will help you remember the information.
> 3. Underline the first letter of each word.
> 4. Create and write a sentence using words that begin with the underlined letters.

Write an acronymic sentence for each of the following sets of information:

1. *Food groups*: meat, dairy, fruit and vegetable, bread and cereal

2. *Meat group*: steak, liver, veal, pork, chicken

3. *Dairy group*: milk, egg, cheese, cream, butter

4. *Fruit and vegetable group*: apple, pear, orange, banana, carrot, bean, radish

5. *Bread and cereal group*: cracker, rice, pasta, granola, muffin, bun, waffle, pancake

Answer the following:

6. What type of information would you try to remember using the acronymic sentence strategy?

Graphic organizers are useful for remembering information that contains a topic, subtopics, and details. Graphic organizers show how information goes together.

Look at the following topic, subtopics, and details and the graphic organizer that goes with them.

Topic: Food Groups

Subtopics and	**Details**
Meat group	steak, pork
Dairy group	milk, cheese
Fruit and vegetable group	apple, pear carrot, radish
Bread and cereal group	cracker, muffin rice, granola

Here is how to use the graphic organizer strategy:

1. Write the topic for the information you need to remember.
2. Underline the subtopics.
3. Circle the details that go with each subtopic.
4. Arrange the topic, subtopics, and details to create a graphic organizer.

---

1. Create a graphic organizer using the following information.

   Topic: Physical Fitness

Subtopics and	**Details**
Agility	speed in changing direction speed in changing body position
Balance	keeping stable body position not falling over
Flexibility	range of motion in a joint
Endurance	continuing activity long time period

2. What type of information would you try to remember using the graphic organizer strategy?

For each of the following write one sentence that tells what should be done when using the strategy:

1. Repetition strategy

2. Forming mind picture strategy

3. Categorization strategy

4. Rhyme strategy

5. Abbreviation strategy

6. Acronym strategy

7. Acronymic sentence strategy

8. Graphic organizer strategy

1-1 Responses will vary.

1-2 Responses will vary.

1-3 Students should write P in front of 3–7. Responses to 9 and 10 will vary.

1-4 Responses will vary for 1 and 2, 4–7.
3. *Things to write with*: pencil, pen, chalk.
Things to write on: paper, chalkboard, cardboard.
Things to read: magazine, book, poem, newspaper.

1-5 1. Harry, Mary, Larry. 2. Larry. 3. Terry Avenue. 4. Harry and Mary's party. 5. Tardy. 6. A sailor. 7. America. 8. 1492. 9. Responses will vary.

1-6 1. pndqd. 2. pnsjm. 3. jsnbn. 4. lcmcg. 5. SGIF. 6. Responses will vary.

1-7 Responses will vary.

1-8 Possible answers: 1. mind. 2. fowl. 3. tale, late. 4–7. Responses will vary.

1-9 Responses will vary.

1-10 1.

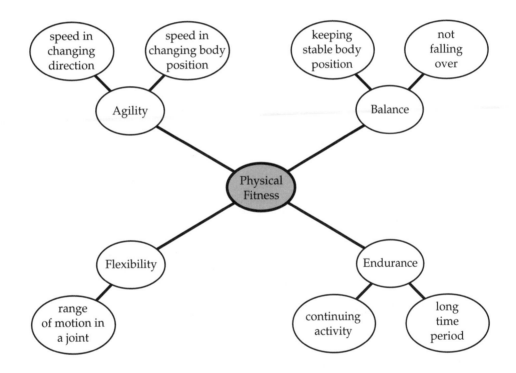

2. Responses will vary.

1-11 Responses will vary but should include the following ideas: 1. Read, write, and recite. 2. Form one or more mind pictures. 3. Place information into categories. 4. Create lines of verse. 5. Use first letters of words to form an abbreviation. 6. Use first letters of words to form a new word. 7. Use the first letter of words to create a sentence. 8. Show how facts are related or organized.

CHAPTER TWO

Reading and Taking Notes from Textbooks

OBJECTIVES

1. Teach students to use the SQRW textbook reading and notetaking strategy.
2. Teach students to apply SQRW to reading assignments in their textbooks.

TITLES OF REPRODUCIBLE ACTIVITIES

USING THE REPRODUCIBLE ACTIVITIES

After you have distributed a reproducible activity, here are suggestions for its use. Feel free to add further information, illustrations, or examples. Wherever possible, relate the activity to actual subject-area assignments.

2-1 Introducing SQRW

Tell students that the formula SQRW stands for the four steps of a strategy for reading and taking notes from textbooks. Introduce students to the words associated with each letter in the strategy. Then have students complete the activity.

2-2 Learning More about SQRW

Use the information in the activity to explain what students are to do for each step of the SQRW strategy. Have students underline the key words that will help them remember what to do for each step.

2-3 Seeing How SQRW Is Used
2-4 Question–Answer Notetaking Form

Have students look at the reading selection on 2-3 as you identify the title, introduction, headings, and conclusion. Have students label each part as you identify them.

Then have students look at the Question–Answer Notetaking Form on 2-4. Explain how the headings in 2-3 were changed into questions using the question-forming words <u>who</u>, <u>what</u>, <u>where</u>, <u>when</u>, <u>why</u>, or <u>how</u>. Point out that not all the question-forming words have to be used for a given reading selection.

Here are the questions created and an explanation of why each was created.

Heading:	Shape
Question:	What is the shape of the earth?
	This question was created from the heading alone.
Question:	What determined the shape of the earth?
	This question was created when additional information was encountered during reading.

Heading:	Mass and Weight
Question:	What is mass?
Question:	How much does the earth weigh?
	These questions were created from the two components of the heading.
Question:	Who was the first person to calculate the mass of earth?
	This question was created when additional information was encountered during reading.

Heading:	Layers
Question:	How many layers does the earth have?
Question:	What are they?
	Both questions were created from the heading alone.

Heading:	Atmosphere
Question:	What is the atmosphere of the earth made of?
	This question was created from the heading alone.
Question:	What keeps the gases near the earth's surface?
	This question was created when additional information was encountered during reading.

Heading:	Changes
Question:	How does the earth change?
	This question was created from the heading alone.
Question:	What is one cause of changes in bodies of water?
Question:	What causes the continents to move?
Question:	How do mountain chains form?
Question:	How do large oceans form?
	These questions were created when additional information was encountered during reading.

2-5 Applying SQRW to a Reading Assignment: "Money"
2-6 Question–Answer Notetaking Form: "Money"

Have students apply what they have learned about SQRW to the reading selection on 2-5 titled "Money." Have students use 2-6 to write their questions and answers. Students may need more than one copy of 2-6 to write their questions and answers.

Tell students that the format they see in 2-6 should be the format they use when writing questions and answers in their own notebooks.

2-7 Applying SQRW to a Reading Assignment: "Amphibians"
2-8 Question–Answer Notetaking Form: "Amphibians"

Have students apply what they have learned about SQRW to the reading selection on 2-7 titled "Amphibians." Have students use 2-8 or their own notebooks to write their questions and answers.

2-9 Chapter Two Mastery Assessment

Have students complete this assessment at any point you believe they have learned to use SQRW. Review the results of the assessment with the students. Provide additional instruction as necessary.

SQRW is a strategy for reading and taking notes from textbooks. Each letter in SQRW stands for a step in the strategy. Read to learn what step in SQRW each letter stands for.

<u>S</u>   stands for   <u>S</u>urvey

<u>Q</u>   stands for   <u>Q</u>uestion

<u>R</u>   stands for   <u>R</u>ead

<u>W</u>   stands for   <u>W</u>rite

1. Write the word that each of these letters stand for.

   S

   Q

   R

   W

2. What combination of letters will help you remember this strategy?

3. When should you use this strategy?

Here is what you should do when you read and take notes from a textbook. As your teacher explains each step, underline the words that will help you remember what to do for that step.

Survey   In this step you read to learn what a textbook reading assignment is about. Here is what to do in this step.

- Read the *title*. It is found at the beginning of the chapter.
- Read the *introduction*. It is usually found in the first paragraph or two of the chapter.
- Read the *headings*. They are found at the beginning of each section of the chapter.
- Examine the *visuals* and read their captions. Visuals are usually found throughout the chapter.
- Read the *conclusion*. It is usually found in the last paragraph or two of the chapter.

Question   In this step you create questions to know what to look for as you read. Here is what to do in this step.

- Use the word *who, what, where, when, why,* or *how* to change each heading into a question. Sometimes you may need to create more than one question for a heading.
- Write the question(s) in your notes. Leave enough space to write the answer(s).

Read   In this step you read to find the answers to the questions you created. Here is what to do in this step.

- Read the question(s) you wrote for the first heading.
- Then read the text that follows the heading to find the answer.
- Do the same thing to find the answers to other questions you wrote.

Write   In this step you write answers to the questions you created. Here is what to do in this step.

- Write the answer below the question in your notes.
- Reread your answer to be sure it is correct.

Look at the reading selection from a textbook as your teacher explains how to use SQRW.

The Earth

The earth is just one of nine planets that revolve around the sun. These planets and the sun form our solar system. The earth is the third closest planet to the sun. It is at the right distance from the sun for the evolution of life as we know it.

Shape

Although the earth appears to be perfectly round in shape, it is not. It is shaped like a ball, but not perfectly. Earth is flatter at the poles than at the equator. The distance around the earth through the north and south poles is approximately 27 miles less than the distance around the earth at the equator. Yet when seen in a photograph from outer space, the earth looks perfectly round. Because of its tremendous size, the bulges at the equator and dips at the poles are not noticed.

The shape of the earth is determined by both gravity and centrifugal force. Gravity pulls everything toward the center of the earth, creating the near ball-like shape. Centrifugal force moves things away from the center of the earth. As the earth revolves, the centrifugal force at the equator is greater than at the poles. This difference in centrifugal force causes the earth to be flatter at the poles than at the equator.

Mass or Weight

The earth is composed of matter. When all the matter is put together, it is called *mass*. The earth's mass or weight is approximately 6,000,000,000,000, 000,000,000 metric tons. This number is read as, "six sextillion metric tons."

Henry Cavendish was the first person to calculate correctly the mass of the earth. He did this sometime during the 1790s, without the benefit of modern equipment. Scientists agree that Henry Cavendish's estimates are very close to today's scientific estimates.

Layers

We know about the earth's surface but much less about what is inside the earth. If the earth were cut in half, you would be able to see three different layers. Near the surface you would see the *crust*. It varies in thickness from 3 miles at the deepest parts of the ocean to 22 miles under the continents.

The second layer you would see is the *mantle*. The mantle goes to a depth of 1,800 miles. Like the crust, it is made of solid rock.

At the center of the earth is the *core*. It is about 2,100 miles in radius. Although the inner core is believed to be solid, it is surrounded by a liquid. The core is mostly iron, with some nickel and silicon.

Atmosphere

The earth is surrounded by a large blanket of air called the *atmosphere*. The atmosphere revolves with the earth. This atmosphere is made of several gases. The most common gases are nitrogen (78%) and oxygen (21%). Gases like carbon dioxide, water vapor, and others make up the remaining one percent.

These gases are held near the earth by gravity. The atmosphere is heavier near the surface of the earth. The air is *heavy* near the surface and gets *thinner* as we move away from the surface into space. Half of the atmosphere is found within 3.5 miles of the earth surface.

Changes

The earth's surface is always changing. The way it looks today is not the way it looked when the earth was formed. Changes come about slowly and are difficult to see in a human lifetime. Sometimes, however, changes come about rapidly, as when Mount St. Helens erupted in 1980 in the Cascade Range located in the southwestern part of the state of Washington.

It is not only the surface of the earth that changes. The continents move and the size of oceans, seas, lakes, and streams changes with them. The crust of the earth sits on six very large plates. These plates move slowly. When they collide, large mountain chains develop. When they move away from each other, large oceans appear.

The earth we know is a very complex environment. It has existed for millions of years and it is constantly changing. The more we know about earth, the better we can adapt to its environment.

Look at the questions and answers as your teacher explains how to use the Question–Answer Notetaking Form.

Title: The Earth

Heading: Shape
Question: What is the shape of the earth?
Answer: Like a ball but not perfectly round
Question: What determined the shape of the earth?
Answer: Gravity and centrifugal force

Heading: Mass and weight
Question: What is mass?
Answer: All matter put together
Question: How much does the earth weigh?
Answer: Approximately six sextillion metric tons
Question: Who was the first person to calculate the mass of earth?
Answer: Henry Cavendish, during the 1790s

Heading: Layers
Question: How many layers does the earth have?
Answer: Three
Question: What are they?
Answer: Surface, mantle, core

Heading: Atmosphere
Question: What is the atmosphere of the earth made of?
Answer: A number of gases: nitrogen 78%, oxygen 21%, other gases 1%
Question: What keeps the gases near the earth's surface?
Answer: Gravity

Heading: Changes
Question: How does the earth change?
Answer: Sometimes slowly, sometimes rapidly as when a volcano like Mount St. Helens erupted
Question: What is one cause of changes in bodies of water?
Answer: Movement of the continents
Question: What causes the continents to move?
Answer: The continents sit on six large plates that move slowly.
Question: How do mountain chains form?
Answer: They form when plates collide.
Question: How do large oceans form?
Answer: They form when plates move away from one another.

Survey the following reading assignment. Create one or more **Questions** for each heading. Write each question on the Question–Answer Notetaking Form provided by your teacher. **Read** to find the answer to each question. **Write** the answer to each question on the Question–Answer Notetaking Form.

Money

Money is some type of paper bill or metal coin that people use to exchange for things they want to purchase or accept for a job that they do. Most modern money consists of paper bills and coins made of copper, nickel, or other metals. Bills and coins from different countries have various appearances and a variety of names.

Uses of Money

Money is used in several ways. The most important function of money is as a medium of exchange. This means that people will accept money in exchange for their goods and services. If money were not available as a medium of exchange, people would have to use the barter system. For example, if you wanted a new jacket, you would have to barter for it by finding something the store owner would accept in exchange, perhaps some vegetables or fruit grown in your garden. Bartering can be inconvenient and time-consuming.

Money also serves as a unit of account. People relate the value of goods and services to a sum of money. In the United States, *dollars* are used to indicate price in the same way that *gallons* are used to measure volume of liquid and *miles* are used to measure distance.

A third function of money is as a way of storing wealth. People are accustomed to saving money to use for future purchases. Stocks, bonds, real estate, gold, and jewels are also considered to be stores of wealth.

Making Money Convenient to Use

Money should be convenient to use. It should be available in pieces of standard value so that the pieces do not have to be weighed or measured individually each time they are needed. It should be carried easily so that people can transport it to purchase what they need. Money should be easily divided into units so that people can make small purchases and receive change if needed. The beads, cocoa beans, salt, shells, and tobacco used in the past for money do not meet the criteria of convenience when applied to modern uses of money.

The Barter System

The barter system of trading was used by most primitive people because they learned by experience that almost everyone was willing to accept certain goods in exchange for products or services. The goods they exchanged included salt, animal hides, cattle, cloth, and articles of gold and silver. These early people used the merchandise they bartered as a medium of exchange in a manner similar to our use of money today.

Coins Come into Use

The Lydians, a people who lived in what is now western Turkey, are credited with the invention of the first metal coins, sometime around 600 B.C. These bean-shaped coins were a natural mixture of gold and silver called *electrum*. The electrum were stamped with a design to show that the King of Lydia guaranteed them to be of uniform size. These coins became a medium of exchange accepted by traders instead of cattle, cloth, or gold dust. When other countries recognized the convenience of the Lydian coins, they devised metal money of their own. Today's coins are modeled after the early Lydian prototypes. Modern coins, not unlike the coins of ancient Lydia, have a government-approved design and a value stamped on their face.

Paper Money Begins to Be Used

Paper money originated in China during the seventh century. Even though the Italian trader, Marco Polo, exposed Europeans to this Chinese innovation, Europeans could not understand how a piece of paper could be valuable. They did not use paper money until the 1600s when banks began to issue paper bills called *bank notes* to depositors and borrowers. The American colonists did not use paper currency. They had to buy products from the English traders with *bills of exchange*. These were documents received from English traders in exchange for goods. It was not until the Revolutionary War that the American Continental Congress issued paper money to help finance this war for independence. From that time forward, the United States used paper money.

Today, it would be very difficult to buy and sell the products available in stores without money. Paper and coin money make it easy and quick to purchase a variety of consumer goods. Imagine what your day would be like if you had to barter for lunch, gasoline, or a ticket to see a movie or sports event.

Question:

Answer:

Question:

Answer:

Question:

Answer:

Question:

Answer:

Question:

Answer:

Question:

Answer:

Question:

Answer:

Question:

Answer:

Question:

Answer:

Question:

Answer:

Amphibians

Amphibians are an interesting class of vertebrate animals from a scientific standpoint. The class Amphibia appeared in the process of evolution between the fishes and the reptiles. They were the first vertebrates to make their way from an aquatic environment to life on land. Amphibians combine characteristics of both land and water animals. The amphibians of today live part of their life on land but must return to the water in order to reproduce.

How Amphibians Evolved

Scientists believe that for millions of years animals lived only in a water environment. There were periodic droughts in which much of the water dried up. Although many varieties of fish existed at this time, only those fish that could withstand drought conditions were able to survive.

The fish that were able to adapt to a drier environment had muscular fins that allowed them to dig deeper into the drying water source. Some were able to move across land from one water hole to another. They often had lungs that allowed them to breathe out of water. The fish who had these land-adaptive characteristics survived the droughts and multiplied to produce new generations of animals. These animals are the ancestors of modern amphibians.

Characteristics of Amphibians

The name *amphibian* comes from the Greek *amphi*, meaning "both," and *bios* meaning "life." This is descriptive of the two stages of existence of amphibians. The young are similar to fish. They can live only in water. As they mature, they change into land-dwelling creatures. Their adult forms combine gills, lungs, fins, and legs.

Amphibians differ from other vertebrates in several ways. They have smooth skin, which is thin and usually moist instead of scales, fur, or feathers. If they have feet, they are webbed. Their toes are soft and do not have claws. The larval forms of the young are usually vegetarian, but the adults are carnivorous. Amphibians breathe with gills, lungs, and skin. They change from a fishlike creature to an animal that can live in water and on land. This is the most unique trait of amphibians.

Classifications

The class *Amphibian* is made up of three distinct *orders*. Order *Apoda* consists of worm-like animals with short or no tails and no legs. They live in tropical areas. Order *Caudata* includes amphibians such as newts and salamanders. These animals have elongated bodies and proportioned tails, usually with two pairs of limbs. The most familiar amphibians belong to the order *Anura*. Frogs and toads and other members of this class have short tailless bodies in their adult stage. They have two pairs of limbs with the hind legs adapted for leaping. Anura have gills in the larval stage and lungs in the adult stage.

Salamanders

One group of Amphibians, the Caudata, are represented primarily by salamanders. Salamanders resemble lizards because they both have long bodies, short legs, and long tails. Salamanders, unlike lizards, have soft moist skin and lack the claws of their reptilian look-alikes.

Salamanders are found in wet or moist areas because they cannot survive where it is dry. These amphibians do not seem to have much protection from predators. They try to protect themselves by giving off a bad-tasting substance and by changing their colors so they are difficult to see.

Frogs and Toads

The most familiar amphibians are the countless frogs and toads found near the ponds and streams in all rural areas of the country. Frogs and toads are similar and are often mistaken for each other. However, they differ in several ways.

The toad enjoys life on land. It begins as an egg fertilized in the water, but soon after hatching it changes from a tadpole to an adult toad. Then it spends most of its time on land. This brown, warty creature returns to the water only to lay its eggs.

Frogs differ from toads in their preference for a watery habitat. Frogs usually live very near water, frequently around ponds and marshes. Bull frogs and leopard frogs are the most common frogs in the United States.

You can see why amphibians are an interesting class of vertebrates. No other animal is as comfortable both in water and on land. Their unique evolution provides a rich field of study for marine scientists.

Question:

Answer:

Question:

Answer:

Question:

Answer:

Question:

Answer:

Question:

Answer:

Question:

Answer:

Question:

Answer:

Question:

Answer:

Question:

Answer:

Question:

Answer:

Next to each letter, write the name of the step in the SQRW strategy. Explain what you should do for each step.

S

Q

R

W

ANSWER KEY FOR CHAPTER TWO

2-1 1. S = Survey, Q = Question, R = Read, W = Write. 2. SQRW. 3. When I need to read assignments in my textbooks.

2-2 Words underlined by students will vary.

2-3 Students label title, introduction, all headings, and conclusion.

2-4 No writing required.

2-5 No writing required.

2-6 Possible questions and answers for each heading are:

Heading:	Uses of Money
Question:	How is money used?
Answer:	Money is used as a medium of exchange, a unit of account, and a store of wealth.

Heading:	Making Money Convenient to Use
Question:	What is done to make money easy to use?
Answer:	It must be available in pieces of standard value, it should be easy to carry, and it should be easy to divide into units.
Question:	What are some examples of things not easy to use as money?
Answer:	Beads, beans, salt, shells, and tobacco

Heading:	The Barter System
Question:	What is the barter system?
Answer:	A way to exchange goods for products or services
Question:	Who used the barter system?
Answer:	Primitive people
Question:	What are examples of goods used in the barter system?
Answer:	Salt, animal hides, cattle, cloth, and articles made of gold or silver

Heading:	Coins Come into Use
Question:	When did coins come into use?
Answer:	Sometime around 600 B.C.
Question:	Who invented coins?
Answer:	The Lydians who lived in what is now western Turkey
Question:	What is "electrum"?
Answer:	A mixture of gold and silver used to make coins
Question:	What is stamped on the face of modern coins?
Answer:	Government-approved design and a value

Heading:	Paper Money Begins to Be Used
Question:	When did paper money begin to be used?
Answer:	The 1600s
Question:	Where did paper money originate?
Answer:	China
Question:	Why didn't the early Europeans use paper money?
Answer:	They could not understand how paper could be valuable.
Question:	When was paper money first used in America?
Answer:	At the beginning of the Revolutionary War

2-7 No writing required.

2-8 Possible questions and answers for each heading are:

Heading:	How Amphibians Evolved
Question:	How did amphibians evolve?
Answer:	They evolved by adapting to a dryer environment caused by droughts.

Question:	What are the characteristics of fish that evolved into amphibians?
Answer:	Muscular fins and lungs

Heading:	Characteristics of Amphibians
Question:	What are the characteristics of amphibians?
Answer:	1. Smooth skin that is thin and moist
	2. Web feet
	3. Soft toes without claws
	4. Vegetarian at birth, but carnivorous as adults
	5. Breathe with gills, lungs, and skin
	6. Live in water and on land

Question:	What is the most distinctive characteristic of amphibians?
Answer:	Their ability to live both in the water and on land
Question:	Where does the word *amphibian* come from?
Answer:	From the Greek words *amphi* and *bios*

Heading:	Classifications
Question:	What are the classifications of amphibians?
Answer:	Apoda, Caudata, Anura

Heading:	Salamanders
Question:	What are salamanders?
Answer:	They are amphibians of the Caudata class.
Question:	What do salamanders resemble?
Answer:	Lizards
Question:	Where can salamanders be found?
Answer:	In wet or moist areas
Question:	How do salamanders protect themselves?
Answers:	They give off a bad-tasting substance and change colors.

Heading:	Frogs and Toads
Question:	What is the difference between frogs and toads?
Answer:	Frogs spend most of their time in or near water. Toads prefer to be on land.
Question:	What are the names of the two most common types of frogs found in the United States?
Answer:	Bullfrogs, leopard frogs

2-9 Students' answers should include information from the following:

Survey:
- Read the title.
- Read the introduction.
- Read the headings.
- Examine the visuals and read their captions.
- Read the conclusion.

Question:
- Use the words *who, what, where, when, why,* or *how* to change each heading into a question. Sometimes you may need to create more than one question for a heading.
- Write the question(s) in your notes. Leave enough space to write the answer.

Read:
- Read the question(s) you wrote for the first heading.
- Then read the text that follows the heading to find the answer.
- Do the same thing to find the answers to other questions you wrote.

Write:
- Write the answer below the question in your notes.
- Reread your answer to be sure it is correct.

Solving Math Word Problems

OBJECTIVES

1. Teach students about the SQRQCQ math word problem-solving strategy.
2. Teach students to apply SQRQCQ to different types of math word problems.

TITLES OF REPRODUCIBLE ACTIVITIES

3-1 Learning about SQRQCQ
3-2 How to Use SQRQCQ
3-3 Practice Using SQRQCQ
3-4 More Practice Using SQRQCQ
3-5 Using SQRQCQ to Solve a Money Problem
3-6 Using SQRQCQ to Solve a Percent Problem
3-7 Using SQRQCQ to Solve a Measurement Problem
3-8 Using SQRQCQ to Solve a Fraction Problem
3-9 On Your Own Using SQRQCQ
3-10 Chapter Three Mastery Assessment
　　　Answer Key

USING THE REPRODUCIBLE ACTIVITIES

After you have distributed a reproducible activity, here are suggestions for its use. Define any terms and clarify any concepts students do not know. Feel free to add further information, illustrations, or examples. Wherever possible, relate the activity to actual subject area assignments.

3-1 Learning about SQRQCQ

Tell students that SQRQCQ is a strategy they should use to solve math word problems. Each letter in SQRQCQ stands for one step in the strategy. Use the following information to teach your students about the steps in the SQCQRQ strategy. Have students write the word that each letter stands for and what each letter reminds them to do.

Survey Read the entire word problem carefully to learn what it is about. If necessary, read it again. Ask your teacher to pronounce or tell you the meaning of any word or term you do not know. Be sure you understand everything in the word problem before you get to the next step.

Question Ask, "What question needs to be answered in the problem?" Think about what the problem is asking. You may find it helpful to form a picture of the problem in your mind or to draw a picture of the problem. Reading the problem out loud may also help you to identify the question.

Read Read to find all the facts you need to answer the question. Look for key words and terms like *how much more, how many were left, all together, total, difference* that can help you to decide which facts are needed to answer the question. Ignore any information that is not needed to answer the question. Cross out any information not needed.

Question Ask, "What computations must I do to answer the question?" Decide if you need to add, subtract, multiply, divide, or do these operations in some combination.

Compute Set up the problem on paper and do the computations. Check to make sure your computations are accurate. Double-check your work. Circle your answer.

Question Ask, "Does my answer make sense?" You can tell if it does by going back and looking at the question you tried to answer. Sometimes you will find that your answer could not be correct because it does not fit the facts in the problem. When this happens, go back through the steps of SQCQRQ until you arrive at an answer that does make sense.

3-2 How to Use SQRQCQ

Use this activity to demonstrate how SQRQCQ is used to solve a math word problem. Have students write the word for each letter in the strategy and what each word reminds them to do.

3-3 Practice Using SQRQCQ
3-4 More Practice Using SQRQCQ

Have students use these activities to practice using SQRQCQ.

3-5 Using SQRQCQ to Solve a Money Problem
3-6 Using SQRQCQ to Solve a Percent Problem
3-7 Using SQRQCQ to Solve a Measurement Problem
3-8 Using SQRQCQ to Solve a Fraction Problem

Have students use these activities to apply SQRQCQ to different types of math word problems.

3-9 On Your Own Using SQRQCQ

Have students work independently to solve the four problems using SQRQCQ.

3-10 Chapter Three Mastery Assessment

Have students complete this assessment at any point you believe they have learned to use the SQRQCQ strategy for solving math word problems presented in this chapter. Review the results of the assessment with students. Provide additional instruction as needed.

The letters SQRQCQ can be used to remember a strategy for solving math word problems. Each letter in SQRQCQ stands for one step in the strategy. As your teacher tells you about SQRQCQ, do the following:

1. Write the word that each letter stands for.
2. Write what each letter reminds you to do.

S

Q

R

Q

C

Q

Read the following math word problem.

> Robert has $650 in the bank. Last year he earned $825 mowing lawns in his neighborhood. This year he expects to increase his business by 20%. Robert wants to know how much money he will earn this year if his business increases as he expects.

Now read to learn how SQRQCQ is used to solve this math word problem.

Survey   **Read to learn about the problem.**
This problem is about Robert and his need to know how much money he will earn this year. If you need to, ask your teacher to tell you the meaning of any words or terms you do not understand. For example, you may need to ask what a 20% increase means.

Question   **Ask, "What question needs to be answered in this problem?"**
Take what you learned about the problem and change it into a question. Sometimes forming a picture in your mind or drawing a picture can help you change the problem into a question.

The question here is:

> How much money will Robert earn next year if his business increases by 20%.

Read   **Read the problem again and write the facts you need to answer the question.**

Here are the facts you should write:

- Robert earned $825 last year.
- He expects his business to increase by 20% this year.

Cross out information not needed to answer the question. Cross out, "Robert has $650 in the bank."

Question   **Ask, "What computations must I do?"**

First, *multiply* $825 by 20%.
Second, add the result to $825.

Compute   **Do the computations on paper. Be sure to check your computations for accuracy. Circle the answer.**

$$\begin{array}{r} \$825 \\ \times \quad .20 \\ \hline \$165.00 \end{array} \qquad \begin{array}{r} \$825 \\ + \quad 165 \\ \hline \$990 \end{array}$$

Question   **Ask, "Does my answer make sense?"**
Look at the question to decide if your answer makes sense. The answer
$990 makes sense because you knew from the key word *increases* that
Robert would make more money this year than last ($825). If your answer
was less than $825, you would know you had done something wrong. You
would then go back through the steps in SQRQCQ to arrive at the correct
answer.

Write the word for which each letter stands. Write a sentence that tells what the letter reminds you
to do.

S

Q

R

Q

C

Q

Use what you have learned about SQRQCQ to solve this math word problem:

Rosa earns $60 a week working at a bookstore. She works 12 hours a week. Rosa has been working at this bookstore for 7 months. Before that, she worked for 4 months in a small pet store. Rosa works 3 days a week at the bookstore. How much money does she earn an hour?

Survey   Read this problem. Write a sentence that tells what this problem is about.

Question   What question needs to be answered in this problem? Write the question.

Read   Write the facts you need to answer the question. Cross out any information in the problem you do not need.

Question   What computations must you do? Write them here.

Compute   Do the computations. Check them for accuracy. Circle your answer.

Question   Does your answer make sense? How do you know?

Use the SQRQCQ strategy to solve the following problem:

Billy's father has been measuring Billy's growth in height. He has been doing this ever since Billy was 5 years old. At that time Billy's height was 35 inches. Billy hopes to grow up to be 6 feet tall. He was 38 inches high at age 6, 42 inches at age 7, and 48 inches at age 8. Today was Billy's ninth birthday. His father measured him and found that Billy had grown 3 inches over the past year. Billy wants to know the average number of inches he has grown over the past 4 years. His father told Billy that he would certainly grow to be 6 feet tall.

S   What is the problem about?

Q   What is the question?

R   Write the facts you need to answer the question. Cross out any information not needed.

Q   What computations must you do?

C   Do the computations. Check them for accuracy. Circle your answer.

Q   Does your answer make sense? Why?

Use SQRQCQ to solve this money problem:

> Alan wanted to buy a new mountain bicycle. He shopped around and found the lowest price to be $460. Alan had $220 in a bank account his parents had started for him. He sold his old bicycle for $35, and got back the $12 his friend Sammy had borrowed two weeks before. The owner of the bicycle shop wanted to know how much more money Alan needed to buy the new bicycle.

S   What is the problem about?

Q   What is the question?

R   Write the facts you need to answer the question. Cross out any information not needed.

Q   What computations must you do?

C   Do the computations. Check them for accuracy. Circle your answer.

Q   Does your answer make sense? Why?

Use SQRQCQ to solve this percent problem:

The town of Newpoint just held an election for mayor. There were 1,256 people in Newpoint who were eligible to vote. Only 634 people voted. Tom Smithson was elected mayor with 65% of the vote. Mary Williams received 22% of the vote, while Ed Adamsley was third with 13% of the vote. Mayor Smithson wanted to know how many people voted for him.

S   What is the problem about?

Q   What is the question?

R   Write the facts you need to answer the question. Cross out any information not needed.

Q   What computations must you do?

C   Do the computations. Check them for accuracy. Circle your answer.

Q   Does your answer make sense? Why?

Use SQRQCQ to solve this measurement problem:

Heidi's brother agreed to build a cage for her parrot. He decided to use wood for the top and bottom of the cage, and wire for the sides. Heidi wanted her parrot to have a lot of room. She asked her brother to build a cage that was 5 feet long, 3 feet wide, and 5 feet high. Heidi's brother wanted to know how many square feet of wood he would need to build the top and bottom of the cage.

S What is the problem about?

Q What is the question?

R Write the facts you need to answer the question. Cross out any information not needed.

Q What computations must you do?

C Do the computations. Check them for accuracy. Circle your answer.

Q Does your answer make sense? Why?

Use SQRQCQ to solve this fraction problem:

José wanted to have a party for his friends. His parents said they would pay for one-third the cost of the party. José spent $41 for snacks, $16 for juice and soda, $7 for decorations, and $8 for plates and cups. Jose's parents wanted to know how much money they owed him for the party.

S   What is the problem about?

Q   What is the question?

R   Write the facts you need to answer the question. Cross out any information not needed.

Q   What computations must you do?

C   Do the computations. Check them for accuracy. Circle your answer.

Q   Does your answer make sense? Why?

Here are some problems for you to solve on your own:

1. Paul's social studies class is studying about elections. He just learned that he must be 18 years old to vote in his state's elections. Paul just turned 11. He wants to know how many years it will be before he can vote in his state.

2. Round Creek is a rapidly growing city. In the last two years its population has grown by 10%. People are moving to Round Creek because of its excellent schools. The current population of Round Creek is 75,383. Its neighbor city of Centerville, six miles down the road, has been dropping in population. It had a population of more than 100,000 before the automobile plant closed. Now it has a population of only 62,129. Determine the difference in current population between these two cities.

3. Ellen lives with her family in Eastern Springs. They will be driving to visit her aunt in Concord, 400 miles away. Ellen's parents plan to visit for three days. They will drive to Concord without stopping for rest. Ellen's father wants to arrive before it gets dark. If they leave Eastern Springs at 9:00 A.M. and drive at an average speed of 50 mph, what time will they arrive in Concord?

4. Emmitt is the star running back on his football team. He has been playing on this team for four years. During this time he has scored 18 touchdowns. Most of his touchdowns were by running, but Emmitt has also caught several passes for touchdowns. Emmitt expects to play football for five more years. His coach is interested in knowing the number of touchdowns Emmitt has averaged a year.

See what you have learned about using SQRQCQ to solve math word problems.

1. The first step in SCRQCQ is **Survey**. What must you do in this step?

2. The second step in SQCQRQ is **Question**. What question should you ask in this step?

3. The third step in SQRQCQ is **Read**. What must you do in this step?

4. The fourth step in SQRQCQ is **Question**. What question should you ask in this step?

5. The fifth step in SQRQCQ is **Compute**. What must you do in this step?

6. The sixth step in SQRQCQ is **Question**. What question should you ask in this step?

7. What should you do if your answer to the question in step 6 is "no"?

3-1 S = Survey. Read to learn about the problem.

Q = Question. Ask what question needs to be answered.

R = Read. Write the facts needed to answer the question.

Q = Question. Ask what computations need to be done.

C = Compute. Do the computations.

Q = Question. Ask if the answer makes sense.

3-2 S = Survey. Read to learn about the problem.

Q = Question. Ask what question needs to be answered.

R = Read. Write the facts needed to answer the question.

Q = Question. Ask what computations need to be done.

C = Compute. Do the computations.

Q = Question. Ask if the answer makes sense.

3-3 Students' answers will vary but should reflect what they learned in 3-1 and 3-2. *Problem answer*: $5 per hour.

3-4 Students' answers will vary but should reflect what they learned in 3-1 and 3-2. *Problem answer*: 4 inches.

3-5 Students' answers will vary but should reflect what they learned in 3-1 and 3-2. *Problem answer*: $193.

3-6 Students' answers will vary but should reflect what they learned in 3-1 and 3-2. *Problem answer*: 412 people.

3-7 Students' answers will vary but should reflect what they learned in 3-1 and 3-2. *Problem answer*: 30 square feet.

3-8 Students' answers will vary but should reflect what they learned in 3-1 and 3-2. *Problem answer*: $24.

3-9 1. 7 years.   2. 13,254.   3. 5:00 P.M.   4. 4.5 touchdowns.

3-10 1. Read to learn about the problem.

2. Ask what question needs to be answered.

3. Write the facts needed to answer the question.

4. Ask what computations need to be done.

5. Do the computations.

6. Ask if the answer makes sense.

7. Go back through the steps to arrive at the correct answer.

Taking Class Notes

OBJECTIVES

1. Teach students the four stages of notetaking.
2. Teach students to take notes.

TITLES OF REPRODUCIBLE ACTIVITIES

4-1 Stages of Notetaking
4-2 First Notes
4-3 Revised Notes
4-4 Remembering Revised Notes
4-5 Words That Tell Something Is Important
4-6 Statements That Tell Something Is Important
4-7 Abbreviating Words
4-8 Abbreviating Statements
4-9 Writing Sentences in a Shorter Way
4-10 Chapter Four Mastery Assessment
Answer Key

USING THE REPRODUCIBLE ACTIVITIES

After you have distributed a reproducible activity, here are suggestions for its use. Feel free to add further information, illustrations, or examples. Wherever possible, relate the activity to actual subject area assignments.

4-1 Stages of Notetaking

Use 4-1 to explain the four stages of notetaking. Have students underline the words that will help them remember what to do for each stage. For Stage 4, review the strategies for remembering information in Chapter One.

4-2 First Notes

Use 4-2 to show students what first notes look like. Use Stage 2 from 4-1 to review what to do when taking first notes.

4-3 Revised Notes

Use 4-3 to show students what revised notes look like. Use Stage 3 from 4-1 to review what to do when revising first notes.

4-4 Remembering Revised Notes

Use 4-4 to review strategies for remembering information as presented in Chapter One.

4-5 Words That Tell Something Is Important

Introduce the signal words *first, second, next,* and *finally*. Tell students these words signal that what follows is important. Have students locate these signal words in "Losing Your Hair." Tell students that teachers use the same words as signals when they speak or lecture. Have students share other signal words they have heard teachers use.

4-6 Statements That Tell Something Is Important

Introduce statements teachers use to signal important information. Review the signal statements provided as examples. Have students add others. Then have students identify signal statements in "The Roman Army."

4-7 Abbreviating Words

Tell students that a good way to increase notetaking speed is by abbreviating words whenever possible. Use the examples to demonstrate how words can be abbreviated. Then have the students complete the activity on their own.

4-8 Abbreviating Statements

Tell students they can sometimes abbreviate entire statements. Use the examples to demonstrate how this is done. Then have students complete the activity.

4-9 Writing Sentences in a Shorter Way

Tell students that speakers usually talk faster than writers write. To capture the important points in a lecture, students should write in short sentences or phrases rather than long sentences. Have students rewrite the long sentences into shorter sentences or phrases.

4-10 Chapter Four Mastery Assessment

Have students complete this assessment at any point you believe they have learned the notetaking skills presented in this chapter. Review the results of the assessment with the students. Provide additional instruction as necessary.

Here are the stages of notetaking. For each stage, there are a number of things you must do. As your teacher explains each stage, underline the words that will help you remember what to do for each stage.

Stage 1: Getting Ready to Take First Notes

1. Have all your notetaking materials ready to use.
2. Review your notes from previous class meetings.
3. Do all assigned readings.

Stage 2: Taking First Notes

1. Write down the important ideas.
2. Write using short sentences, phrases, abbreviations, and symbols.
3. Leave space between new ideas.
4. Copy what your teacher writes on the chalkboard.
5. Draw a **circle** around any word you write whose meaning you do not know. Also write the word in the section called "New Words to Learn."
6. Place a **?** in front of information you write in your notes but do not understand.

Stage 3: Writing Revised Notes

1. Use a dictionary or the glossary to learn the meaning of any word you circled in your first notes. Write the meaning of the word in the "New Words to Learn" section.
2. Ask your teacher to explain anything you marked with a ? in your first notes. Revise that part of your notes to include what you learned from your teacher.
3. Expand the short sentences, phrases, abbreviations, and symbols in your first notes into longer and more complete statements.

Stage 4: Remembering Your Revised Notes

1. Select strategies you can use to remember the information in your revised notes for a test.
2. Use these strategies as often as needed to remember the information.

Class: Geography   **Period:** 4th   **Date:** 5/23/97   **Page:** 1

Topic: Deserts Around the World

Types
? →   Hot deserts; high temps—75+°
      Cold deserts; low temps—belo 45°

Location
      Hot—betw 15° & 45° N/S equator; subtropics
      Cold—above 60° long. N/S equator; arctic, antarctic

Characteristics
      Little H_2O
      Some sandy
      Some rocky & no sand
      Some flat, some mountainous

Causes of (desertification)
      Weather
         Little rain
         Warm winds
      People
         Firewood
         Fields
      (Domesticated) animals (overgraze)

Animal life
      Many do not drink H_2O
? →   Some go w/out water for wks
      Arabian camel good example

New Words to Learn

desertification
domesticated
overgraze

Class: Geography   **Period:** 4th   **Date:** 5/23/97   **Page:** 1

Topic: Deserts Around the World

Types
  Some deserts are called hot deserts because the temperatures during the daytime are 75 degrees or higher.
  Some deserts are called cold deserts because the temperatures are below 45 degrees most of the time.

Location
  Hot deserts are found in the subtropics both north and south of the equator. Most are found north and south of the equator ranging between 15 and 45 degrees longitude.

Characteristics
  Little water is found in the desert.
  Some deserts are sandy but not all of them.
  Some deserts are mostly rocks with no sand.
  Some deserts are flat and some are mountainous.

Causes of desertification
  Weather can cause desertification. Areas that receive little rain and are covered by warm winds that suck what little water there is from the soil and plants end up as deserts.

  People can cause desertification too. Cutting trees for firewood and clearing out forests to make fields for planting crops or raising domesticated animals that overgraze can produce deserts.

Animal life
  Some animals live in the desert even though there is little water to drink. These animals get their water from their food. Desert animals can often go for weeks without water. The Arabian camel is a good example of a desert animal that can go many days without water.

New Words to Learn

domesticated: Animals raised on ranches and farms.
overgrazed: Overuse of fields by animals.
desertification: Turning forests and farmlands into deserts by using poor forest and farm-land management techniques.

Read about the strategies you can use to remember the information in your revised notes. Listen as your teacher describes each strategy. Use the space below each strategy to write key words or ideas to help you remember the strategy.

Repetition is a strategy in which you read, write, and recite information.

Mind picture is a strategy in which you form one or more pictures in your mind.

Categorization is a strategy in which you place information into categories.

Rhyme is a strategy in which you create lines of verse.

Abbreviation is a strategy in which you use the first letter of words to form an abbreviation.

Acronym is a strategy in which you use the first letter of words to form a pronounceable word.

Acronymic sentences is a strategy in which you use the first letter of words to create a sentence.

Graphic organizer is a strategy in which you show how facts are related or organized.

Words That Tell Something Is Important

During a lecture, your teacher often will use words that tell you something is important for you to write in your notes. These words are called **signal words**. If you listen for signal words, you will be more likely to write down important information.

Here are some signal words used by teachers.

first   second   next   finally

Read the following lecture. The topic is "Losing Your Hair." As you read the lecture, see how these signal words call your attention to important information. Circle each of these signal words as you read the lecture.

Losing Your Hair

As people get older they typically lose some of their hair. Men usually lose their hair at an earlier age than women. However, there are many bald women just as there are bald men. People don't like to lose their hair because they think it makes them look older. There are several things that can be done to stop the loss of hair. The first thing most people try is to take better care of their hair by regular shampooing. There are many different types of shampoos available, many of which promise to stop the loss of hair. The second remedy is to massage the scalp regularly with a stiff brush or with one's fingers. When this doesn't work, the next thing people usually try is a vitamin therapy. There are many different vitamins that are thought to encourage hair growth.

Finally, when all else fails, people go out and buy a wig or toupee. Both are used to cover part or all of the scalp. As you see, it is natural to lose hair, but there are things you can do to keep that "young look."

Write a paragraph on this topic. Use signal words in your paragraph.

What to Do to Be a Good Student

Statements That Tell Something Is Important

Teachers often use signal statements to tell you something is important for you to write in your notes. Teachers use signal statements that look much like these:

"Here is something you should know."
"I wouldn't forget this point if I were you."
"Remember this."
"This is particularly important."
"There are five things you have to know."

Read the following lecture. The topic is "The Roman Army." As you read the lecture, look for signal statements that call your attention to important information. Circle each signal statement as you read the lecture.

The Roman Army

The expansion of Rome made possible in part by the courage and skill of its soldiers. Be sure to remember that the Roman army became a match for any army in the Western world. The Roman army was made up mostly of foot soldiers. In early times, the soldiers were organized into groups of 8,000 called phalanxes. Make sure that you know that a phalanx was a group of soldiers massed together with shields joined and spears overlapping. Later the army replaced phalanxes with legions. A legion was made up of 3,600 men. Write in your notes that the legion was much more effective in battle than a phalanx. Roman soldiers were tough, loyal, practical men. The major thing to know is that they could handle just about any task from repairing weapons to sewing their own clothes. They had to obey rules or face a very severe punishment. The most important point is that because of its great army, Rome took over all of Italy. I am going to expect you to know that when the Roman army began to weaken, Rome began to lose its control of Italy.

Think of two signal statements you use when you are talking to someone. Write them here.

Abbreviating Words

It is important to write first notes quickly. A good way to increase your notetaking speed is to write using abbreviations. An abbreviation is a short way of writing something. Here are some words and the abbreviations that can be used to write them.

Words	*Abbreviations*	*Words*	*Abbreviations*
psychology	psy	medicine	med
English	Eng	diameter	dia
month	mo	year	yr
vocabulary	vocab	Florida	Fl

Here are some words you may have to write when taking notes. For each word, write an abbreviation. You can make up any abbreviation for a word as long as it allows you to recognize the word.

November

amendment

general

Africa

William

science

interest

library

kidney

history

computer

geography

Another good way to increase your notetaking speed is to abbreviate statements you hear and want to write in your first notes. For example, you can abbreviate *grade point average* as *gpa* or *home computer* as *ho comp*.

You can also abbreviate the names of organizations or titles. For example, *Federal Bureau of Investigation* is commonly abbreviated *FBI*. The *chief executive officer* of a company is commonly abbreviated *CEO*.

Create an abbreviation for each of the following:

Organization of American States

Republic of China

mathematics teacher

football coach

weekly assignment

National Aeronautics and Space Agency

North Atlantic Treaty Organization

shopping list

longitude and latitude

Saturday afternoon and evening

television program

World Wide Web

pencil and paper

When you take first notes, you should use phrases or short sentences as often as possible. For example, instead of writing the long sentence, "As air cools it loses its ability to hold water vapor," you could write, "Cool air can't hold water vapor."

For each sentence below, rewrite the sentence in a shorter form or as a phrase.

1. As we have noted, the Constitution gives to each branch of the government its own distinctive field of governmental authority: legislative, executive, and judicial.

2. The weight at which you look and feel most comfortable is your "ideal" weight or the healthiest weight for your body.

3. Any water used for drinking purposes not only must be free of salt but also should be free of foreign matter.

4. The common cold is really a group of symptoms and signs caused by a variety of viruses.

5. Each of the American colonies was born out of a particular set of circumstances, and so each had its own character.

Show what you have learned about taking notes in class. Write what you have learned to do in each stage of taking notes.

Stage 1: Getting Ready to Take First Notes

Stage 2: Taking First Notes

Stage 3: Writing Revised Notes

Stage 4: Remembering Your Revised Notes

4-1 Words underlined by students will vary.

4-2 No responses required.

4-3 No responses required.

4-4 Key words or ideas written by students will vary.

4-5 Students should circle signal words in the lecture: *first, second, next, finally*. Students' paragraphs will vary in content but should include signal words.

4-6 Signal statements students should circle are:

"Be sure to remember"
"Make sure that you know"
"Write in your notes"
"The major thing to know"
"The most important point"
"I am going to expect you to know"

Signal statements written by students will vary.

4-7 Responses will vary.

4-8 Responses will vary.

4-9 Responses will vary.

4-10 Students' responses should include the ideas presented in 4-1.

CHAPTER FIVE

Using the Library

OBJECTIVES

1. Teach students to use the library to find information.
2. Teach students to evaluate the information they find.

TITLES OF REPRODUCIBLE ACTIVITIES

USING THE REPRODUCIBLE ACTIVITIES

After you have distributed a reproducible activity, here are suggestions for its use. Define any terms and clarify any concepts students do not know. Feel free to add further information, illustrations, or examples. Wherever possible, relate the activity to actual subject-area assignments.

5-1 A Strategy for Using the Library

Today's library contains a mix of traditional print and newer electronic resources. Libraries vary in the specific products they purchase, but the strategy for using the library remains constant.

Use this activity to take students through the steps for using a library. Use the acronym IFES to help students remember the steps. Consider inviting the librarian to your class to discuss with students how today's library contains information in both print and electronic form. Then have students answer the questions on their own.

5-2 Formats of Information

Libraries have materials in many different formats. Review the four formats of information with students. Describe the kind of equipment that may be needed to use information stored in each format. Bring samples to the classroom to show to students. Then have students complete the activity.

5-3 Books and Other Materials Found in a Library

Many students associate books with the library. Libraries contain many different types of materials. Students need to know how to find and use the many different types of materials in a library.

Have students complete the activity to tell what types of materials they have used in a library. Provide examples of materials that students have not used.

5-4 Learning about Card and Online Catalogs

You may want to invite the librarian to your class for this activity.

Libraries today are converting their card catalogs to online catalogs. Many libraries no longer have a card catalog, but some still do. Larger libraries may still have a card catalog for a specific collection within the library, or for older materials. An online catalog in one library can be very different from an online catalog in another library. Not only may it be searched differently, but the information included may be different. Some include only records for the materials owned by the library. Some may not include certain types of materials, such as newspapers. Others include connections to electronic databases of magazine articles. Still others provide connections to the Internet.

Use this activity to teach students about the catalogs in your library. Ask the librarian to explain the difference between a card catalog and an online catalog. Then have students ask the librarian the questions necessary to complete the activity.

5-5 Learning about a Card Catalog

Use this activity even if your school does not have a card catalog. Your students may use other local libraries that still have card catalogs. If they do, they need to know about the three types of cards found in the card catalog.

Explain why three cards are necessary. Be sure to point out that the author card includes a list of subjects for this book at the bottom of the card. Tell students that the number in the upper left-hand corner is the call number. Tell students you will be teaching them about call numbers later on (5-10). Then have students answer the questions.

5-6 Using a Card Catalog

Use this activity only if your library has a card catalog.

Have students look up the subject *endangered species* in the card catalog. Tell them to select one book owned by the library on this subject and use it to answer the questions.

5-7 Learning about an Online Catalog

Use this activity even if your school does not have an online catalog. Your students may use other local libraries that have online catalogs. If they do, they need to know about records in an online catalog.

All online catalogs have records of items owned by the library. The information about each item is arranged on the record in fields. Different online catalogs may present the information in different ways, but the fields of information included are always the same. For example, some catalogs use the word *subjects* and others use the word *descriptors*. Some online catalogs do not label the field name. The record may look just like a record in the card catalog.

Use this activity to explain to students the type of information found on a record. Then have students answer the questions about the sample record. You may bring copies of a record from your online catalog for students to compare.

5-8 Using an Online Catalog

Use this activity only if your library has an online catalog.

Have students look up the subject *space flight to the moon* in the online catalog. Tell them to select one book owned by the library on this subject and use it to answer the questions.

5-9 Learning about the Dewey Decimal System

The Dewey Decimal System is a numeric classification system used by most school and public libraries. Academic libraries use a different system (Library of Congress). A classification system does two things: it brings together books on related topics so that they can be shelved near each other on library shelves, and it assigns a unique number to each book so that it can be located on the shelf.

Review the ten major classes of the Dewey Decimal System with students. Explain to students that books on similar topics will be found near each other on the shelf. Define for students any terms they do not understand. Then have students complete the activity.

5-10 Finding Books by Call Number

The Dewey Decimal System uses numbers that include decimals. The first line is a whole number and the second line is a decimal number. Use the example to show students that the call number $\frac{636}{.71}$ is the same as 636.71.

Review decimals as necessary. Then use the example to show students how call numbers in the Dewey Decimal System are arranged in numerical order. Have students complete the Dewey Decimal ordering activity.

5-11 Learning about Electronic Databases

Electronic databases are computerized versions of print indexes. Print indexes and electronic databases are used to identify citations in magazines, journals, and newspapers by topic. Print indexes have been around for more than a hundred years, but libraries are buying more and more indexes in electronic format as databases. These databases may be on CD ROM, online as part of a larger computer that you connect to, or on the Internet. Many of the Internet-based databases are on the World Wide Web. Libraries pay for subscriptions to these databases, even if they are on the WWW. They are not free.

There are many different electronic database products available for libraries to purchase. Some include citations and abstracts only, others include the full text of the article. Some cover all topics, some include only newspapers, and still others identify magazines in a specific subject. Find out about the electronic databases available in your library before you have students complete this activity. You may wish to invite the librarian to your class for this activity.

Explain to students that they use an electronic database to identify articles in newspapers and magazines. Point out that many school and public libraries have electronic databases. Have students read about electronic databases and answer the questions.

5-12 Using an Electronic Database

Use this activity even if your school does not have an electronic database for magazine or newspaper articles. Your students may use other local libraries that have electronic databases. If they do, they need to know about records in an electronic database.

Electronic databases have a record for each article in the database. Here is the record from the activity. On the record, the information is arranged in fields. There are six fields in this record. Each field has information about the article.

Sample CD ROM Record   Copyright © 1996 by UMI Company. All rights reserved.

Access No.:	02229175 ProQuest Periodical Abstracts - Library
Title:	July 20, 1969: The greatest adventure
Authors:	Keefe, Ann
Journal:	Cobblestone: The History Magazine for Young People
	ISSN: 0199-5197 Jrnl Group: Academic
	Vol: 16 Iss: 1 Date: Jan 1995 p: 36–41
	Type: Feature Length: Long
	Illus: Photograph; Illustration
Subjects:	History; Space exploration; Moon
Abstract:	The dialogue between the astronauts and launch control at Cape Kennedy during the first landing on the moon on July 20, 1969 is presented. The adventure marked a significant moment in history.

Each field is labeled. Explain to students what information is in each field.

Access No. includes the access number and name of the database.
Title is the title of the article.

Authors identifies the author(s) of the article.
Journal identifies the journal name and citation for the article.
Subjects shows the subjects used to index the article.
Abstract includes a summary of the article.

Have students answer the questions about the sample record.

Because records vary from database to database, you may want to extend this activity by inviting the librarian to your classroom to show students sample records from a variety of databases.

5-13 Learning about Print Indexes

Print indexes are used to identify articles in magazines, journals, and newspapers by topic. One of the most common print indexes is the *Readers' Guide to Periodical Literature*. Although many libraries now own electronic databases, some may only have print indexes.

Print indexes are still necessary to use to find articles in older publications. For example, if you want to find an article about *man's first steps on the moon* in a magazine from that year, you will probably have to use a print index. Most electronic databases only go back to the 1980s, and many libraries only buy the current years. Print indexes, however, go back as far as the nineteenth century.

Also, print indexes are available for specific disciplines. For example, if your library has the *Art Index* only in print, and you need information in art magazines, it may be a better index to use than an electronic one that may include only a few art magazines.

Tell students that some libraries may not have electronic databases. When this is the case, they must use a print index. Have students read about print indexes and answer the questions.

5-14 Using a Print Index

Print indexes, like electronic databases, include citations to articles from a specific list of magazine, journal, and newspaper titles covered by the index. The list of titles covered by the index can be found at the front of the book. Your library may not own all of the magazines, journals, and newspapers covered by the index.

Some print indexes abbreviate the title of the publication. The list at the front of the index will also include the abbreviation for the title used in the citation. The example in this activity is from the *Readers' Guide to Periodical Literature*, which abbreviates most titles. Note that the magazine title used in one of the examples, *Time*, however, is not abbreviated. Shorter titles usually are not abbreviated.

Use the labeled example to review the parts of a citation with students. Review the four steps to follow when using a print index. Explain that the library may not own all the magazines for the citations they find, and offer suggestions for what they can do when that happens (e.g., select another citation, look in another library). Then direct students to label the parts of the citation provided.

5-15 Locating Electronic Databases and Print Indexes

Use the activity to have students locate specific electronic databases and the print indexes available in your library. Arrange a schedule with your librarian so students can complete the activity.

5-16 Learning about Keywords
5-17 Learning about Boolean Connectors

Every kind of database used to find information requires keywords and knowledge of Boolean connectors. Online catalogs, electronic databases for articles, multimedia reference sources such as encyclopedias, even searches on the World Wide Web require students to select keywords and put them together in a computer search using Boolean connectors.

Activity 5-16 introduces students to keywords. Because computers are very literal, an efficient computer search requires students to use all possible keywords, forms of the keyword (e. g., plural, tense), and synonyms or related words.

Explain keywords to students and have them read through the example provided. Then have students select two keywords from the topic provided. Have students complete the activity by placing the keywords in the box and writing other forms for each keyword as well as synonyms or related words. Help students brainstorm for words to place in the box, emphasizing the need for creativity.

Activity 5-17 shows how Boolean connectors are used to do a computer search with keywords. Use the Venn diagrams to explain the three Boolean connectors **and, or, not**. Have students complete the activity by drawing Venn diagrams for each connector.

5-18 Evaluating Sources of Information

The availability of information from a wide variety of sources underscores the importance of teaching students how to evaluate the believability of sources. Tell students that information comes from people, not from a medium such as a computer, and they must evaluate the believability of the *source* of the information and not the medium through which it was presented.

Have students brainstorm and write down sources of information they can find at home and at school. Then have them rate the believability of each source using the scale provided. Lead a class discussion about why students rate some sources as more believable than others.

5-19 What Makes Information Believable

Students should use the six rules to decide if information is believable. The acronym TRACKS can help students remember these six rules.

Review the six rules for deciding if information is believable. Explain any terms or concepts that students do not understand. Then have students complete the activity by reading each example and rating it as Believable, Sometimes Believable, or Not Believable.

Finally, have students return to 5-18 and change any of their ratings based on what they have learned.

5-20 Chapter Five Mastery Assessment

Have students complete this assessment at any point you believe they have learned to use the library to locate and evaluate information. Review the results of the assessment with students. Provide additional instruction as needed.

The library is a good place to look for information. Librarians are there to help you. Most libraries have computers you can use to find information. Here are the steps that will help you remember a strategy for using the library.

Step 1: Identify sources you can use to obtain information in the library.

Step 2: Find the sources of information you need to complete your assignment.

Step 3: Evaluate the believability of the information you find.

Step 4: Select the information that is most believable to complete your assignment.

The acronym **IFES** will help you remember the steps in the strategy for using the library.

1. What does the letter **I** remind you to do?

2. The letter **F?**

3. **E?**

4. **S?**

Information in a library is packaged in many different ways. The way information is packaged is called its **format**. Four major formats are:

Print	Print format uses paper. Examples are books, magazines, and newspapers.
Electronic	Electronic formats use a computer to deliver information. Electronic formats include CD ROM and the Internet.
Audio visual (A/V)	A/V formats require you to watch or listen. Examples include audio cassettes, video cassettes, and films.
Microform	Microform (micro-format) makes an image smaller and puts it on plastic to be read in a machine. Microfilm, microfiche, and micro cartridge are examples of microforms.

Write the name of the format that goes with each illustration:

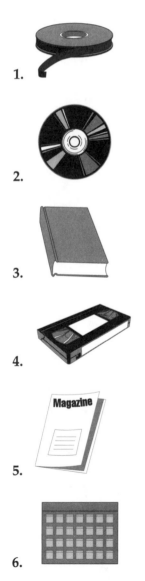

1.

2.

3.

4.

5.

6.

Read to learn about books and other materials found in a library. Place a ✔ in front of each that you have used in your library.

_____ **Books:** In-depth coverage of a subject printed on paper and bound together in a single volume.

_____ **Reference sources:** Materials to help you do research, such as encyclopedias, almanacs, and atlases. Usually these materials cannot be taken from the library.

_____ **Newspapers:** Daily publications containing news and opinions about current events, feature stories, and advertisements.

_____ **Magazines:** Weekly or monthly publications with articles on topics of general interest. Magazines usually contain glossy pictures and advertisements.

Books, reference sources, newspapers, and magazines may be found in the following **formats**. Place a ✔ in front of each format you have used in your library.

_____ **Print:** Sheets of paper, sometimes bound with a soft or hard cover.

_____ **Microfiche:** Flat plastic cards with images that are made smaller, read or copied on reader/printers.

_____ **Microfilm:** Small reels of film with images that are made smaller, read or copied on reader/printers.

_____ **Video cassette:** Cartridge containing tape with a filmed or televised image, usually including sound, and viewed using a television monitor and VCR.

_____ **Audio cassette:** Small cartridge containing tape with recorded speech or sounds and listened to using a tape recorder.

_____ **CD ROM** (Compact Disc Read Only Memory): A computer-based method of storing information as a database, requiring a computer and CD player for use.

_____ **Multimedia:** Database that uses full text, video, sound, animation, and other features to provide information.

All libraries have one or more catalog listing materials found in the library. Some libraries have a **card catalog** where the information about each item is typed on a card and filed alphabetically in drawers in a cabinet. Most libraries have an **online catalog** where the information about each item is stored in a computer. Some libraries have both a card catalog and an online catalog.

Use the information provided by your librarian to answer the questions.

1. Does your library have a card catalog?   Yes   No

   If yes, circle the items that you can find using your library's card catalog.

   books   magazines   video cassettes

   audio cassettes   newspapers

2. Does your library have an online catalog?   Yes   No

   If yes, does your online catalog have a name?   Yes   No

   Write its name here:

3. Circle each of the following you can do using your library's online catalog.

   Connect to the Internet   Identify articles in
                                                magazines and/or newspapers

   Connect to other libraries   Use an encyclopedia or
                                                other reference source

4. Write what have you learned about the card catalog and/or online catalog in your library.

Each item owned by the library has three cards in the card catalog. You may look for an item by **subject**, **title**, or **author**. Look at the sample cards from a card catalog. The sample cards are for a book.

Subject Card

SPACE FLIGHT TO THE MOON—HISTORY.

629.454097   Chaikin, Andrew, 1956-

A man on the moon : the voyages of the Apollo astronauts

Title Card

A man on the moon : the voyages of the Apollo astronauts

629.454097   Chaikin, Andrew, 1956-

A man on the moon : the voyages of the Apollo astronauts

Author Card

629.454097   Chaikin, Andrew, 1956–
A man on the moon : the voyages of the Apollo astronauts /
Andrew Chaikin.
--New York, N.Y. : Viking, 1994.
xv, 670 p., <16> p. of plates : ill. ; 24 cm.

Includes bibliographical references (p. 601-605) and index.

ISBN 0670814466

1. Project Apollo (U.S.)--History. 2. Space flight to the
moon--History.   I. Title.

Use the information on the cards to answer the questions:

1. What is the title of this book?

2. Who is the author?

3. Under what subjects can you look to find this book?

4. When was this book published?

5. What is the name of the publisher?

6. How many pages are there in this book?

Use the card catalog in your library to find a book under the subject *endangered species*. Answer the following questions about the book you find:

1. What is the title of the book?

2. Who is the author?

3. Under what other subjects can you look to find this book?

4. When was this book published?

5. What is the name of the publisher?

6. How many pages are there in the book?

7. Write the number that tells where this book is located on the shelf in the library.

Each item owned by the library has one **record** in the online catalog. The record has all the information you need to identify the book and find it in the library. Look at this sample computer record from an online catalog. The sample record is for a book.

Author:	Breuer, William B., 1923—
Title:	Race to the moon : America's duel with the Soviets / William B. Breuer.
Published:	Westport, Conn. : Praeger, 1993.
Call Number:	629.454
Description:	x, 222 p., <18> p. of plates : ill. ; 25 cm.
ISBN:	0275944816 (alk. paper)
Notes:	Includes bibliographical references (p. <215>-216) and index.
Subjects:	Project Apollo (U.S.)
	Space flight to the moon--History.
	Rocketry--Research--Germany--History.

Use the information on the record to answer the questions.

1. Under what subjects can you look to find this book?

2. What is the title of this book?

3. Who is the author?

4. When was this book published?

5. What is the name of the publisher?

6. How many pages are there in this book?

7. Does the book have any illustrations?

8. What is the call number for this book?

Use the online catalog in your library to find a book under the subject *space flight to the moon*. Answer the following questions about the book you find:

1. What is the title of the book?

2. Who is the author?

3. Under what other subjects can you look to find this book?

4. When was this book published?

5. What is the name of the publisher?

6. How many pages are there in the book?

7. Does the book have any illustrations?

8. What is the call number for the book?

Many school and public libraries use the Dewey Decimal System. Books on similar subjects are shelved together under ten main classes. Here are the ten main classes and the numbers that go with each.

000–099	Generalities	500–599	Pure Science
100–199	Philosophy and Related Areas	600–699	Technology (Applied Sciences)
200–299	Religion	700–799	The Arts
300–399	The Social Sciences	800–899	Literature and Rhetoric
400–499	Language	900–999	General Geography, History, etc.

Under which numbers would you find books on the following topics:

1. biology

2. countries in Africa

3. space flight to the moon

4. Spanish terms and expressions

5. A general encyclopedia

6. Catholic Church

7. the Greek philosopher Aristotle

8. the writer Mark Twain

9. American government

10. the composer Beethoven

Finding Books by Call Number

Most school libraries use the Dewey Decimal System of call numbers. Call numbers are used to locate books on library shelves. When you look at a call number on the spine of a book, it will look like this: 751 .71 but think of it as 751.71.

Look at these call numbers to see how they have been placed in correct order from left to right.

636	636	636	636	636	636
.7	.708	.72	.73	.737	.752

The following call numbers are not in correct order.

751	751	752	751	751	751
.73	.422		.4	.45	.4225

Write them in their correct order here.

Electronic databases are used to identify articles in magazines and newspapers. On a computer, you can obtain a summary of an article. This summary is called an **abstract**. Sometimes you can also obtain the entire article. An entire article is called **full text**.

Electronic databases are available in these formats: **CD ROM** databases, **online** databases, and on the **Internet**. Ask your teacher or librarian which of these formats are found in your library.

Answer these questions.

1. What do you use electronic databases to identify?

2. In what formats will you find electronic databases?

3. In what formats are electronic databases found in your school?

4. What is an abstract?

5. What is full text?

An electronic database provides records for articles found in magazines and newspapers. A record contains all the information needed to find an article. The electronic database includes the abstract of an article and sometimes the full text. The information in the sample record is for a magazine article.

Sample CD ROM Record   Copyright © 1996 by UMI Company.

Access No.:	02229175 ProQuest Periodical Abstracts—Library
Title:	July 20, 1969: The greatest adventure
Authors:	Keefe, Ann
Journal:	Cobblestone: The History Magazine for Young People
	ISSN: 0199-5197 Jrnl Group: Academic
	Vol: 16 Iss: 1 Date: Jan 1995 p: 36–41
	Type: Feature Length: Long
	Illus: Photograph; Illustation
Subjects:	History; Space exploration; Moon
Abstract:	The dialogue between the astronauts and launch control at Cape Kennedy during the first landing on the moon on July 20, 1969 is presented. The adventure marked a significant moment in history.

Use the sample record to answer these questions.

1. What is the title of this article?

2. In what magazine was this article published?

3. When was the article published?

4. What is the name of the database used to access this record?

5. What is the article about?

6. Who wrote the article?

7. How long is the article?

If your library does not have an electronic database, use a print index to identify articles in magazines and newspapers. Print indexes look like books. The name of a commonly used print index is *The Readers' Guide to Periodical Literature*. The *Readers' Guide* can be used to locate articles on any topic. Most libraries also have print indexes you can use to locate articles in a specific subject area, such as science.

1. What do you use to identify articles in magazines and newspapers if your library does not have an electronic database?

2. What is *The Readers' Guide to Periodical Literature*?

3. What is the difference between *The Readers' Guide to Periodical Literature* and a specific subject index?

4. Have you found print indexes to be helpful? Why?

A print index contains citations to articles in magazines or newspapers. Each citation includes the information you need to find an article about a topic. Here is an example of a citation with its parts labeled.

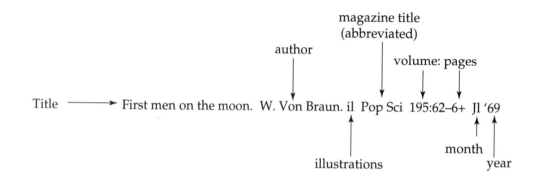

Follow these steps when using a print index to locate information about a topic.

1. Look up a topic in the current volume.
2. Identify citations related to the topic.
3. If the title of a magazine or newspaper is abbreviated, look in the front of the index to find the complete title.
4. Check to see which magazines or newspapers included in the citations are available in your library.

Label each part of the following citation.

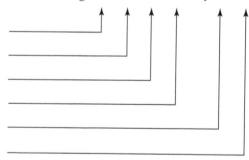

Giant leap for mankind; first moon landing. il Time 94:10–12+ Jl 25 '69

Locating Electronic Databases and Print Indexes

Go to your library and ask your librarian to help you locate electronic databases and print indexes. Then complete the following.

1. The title of an electronic database for magazine articles in my library is:

2. The title of an electronic database for newspaper articles in my library is:

3. Another interesting electronic database I found in my library is:

4. An important print index in my library is:

You need a keyword to do a computer search on a topic. A keyword is an important word about your topic. Because computers do exactly what you tell them to do, you will usually need more than one keyword to locate all the records with information on your topic.

For example, if you ask the computer to search for the keyword **child**, it will find all records that contain the word **child**. It will *not* find records that contain other forms of **child**, such as **childhood** or **children**. It will *not* find records that contain synonyms for **child**, such as **youngster**, or related words, such as **boy** or **girl**.

Here is an example of how to search using the keyword **child** and its other forms, synonyms, and related words.

child or children or childhood or youngster or boy or girl

In the box, write two words that can be used as keywords for the following topic:

How insects can help plants.

For each keyword, write as many other forms of the keyword as you can. Do the same for synonyms and related words.

	1	**2**
Keywords		
Other Forms of Keyword		
Synonyms and Related Words		

Boolean connectors are used to search for information in online catalogs, electronic databases, and on the World Wide Web (WWW). The three Boolean connectors are: **and**, **or**, and **not**. The diagrams illustrate how they are used.

Connector	Use	Example	Diagram
and	Focus or Narrow a search	exploring and moon	
or	Expand or Broaden a search	exploring or exploration	
not	Exclude specific words	not shuttle	

Will find computer records with the word *exploring* **and** the word *moon* in them.

Will find computer records with the word *exploring* **or** the word *exploration* in them.

Will **not** find any computer records with the word *shuttle* in them.

Draw the diagram that illustrates each connector:

1. oceans or lakes

2. children and games

3. planets not Mars

Where does information come from? Every day you acquire information from various sources. Think about the sources of information you can find at home and in school. Write as many as you can.

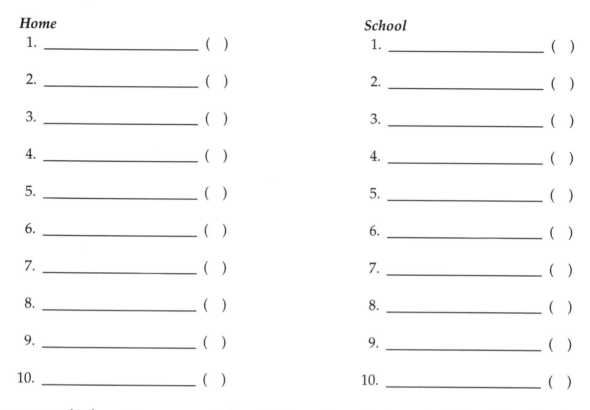

Home

1. _____ ( )

2. _____ ( )

3. _____ ( )

4. _____ ( )

5. _____ ( )

6. _____ ( )

7. _____ ( )

8. _____ ( )

9. _____ ( )

10. _____ ( )

School

1. _____ ( )

2. _____ ( )

3. _____ ( )

4. _____ ( )

5. _____ ( )

6. _____ ( )

7. _____ ( )

8. _____ ( )

9. _____ ( )

10. _____ ( )

Some sources of information are more **believable** than others. Evaluate the believability of each source you listed by rating each source on the following scale. Write the number for your rating inside the ( ).

1 Not Believable
2 Possibly Believable
3 Believable

Read each rule for deciding if information is believable. Then read about the source of information presented with the rule. Write 1, 2, or 3 in front of each source to show how believable it is based on the rule.

     1   Not Believable
     2   Possibly Believable
     3   Believable

1. The information is **Timely**.

_____ A video about nuclear energy produced in 1968.

2. The information appears in a **Reputable** source.

_____ A research article about aerobics in *The Journal of Exercise Physiology*.

3. The information is **Accurate**.

_____ A newspaper article describing the 64 states of the United States.

4. The information is **Consistent** with what other experts say about the topic.

_____ An essay arguing that the sun revolves around the moon.

5. The information is written by one or more persons **Knowledgeable** in the field.

_____ A magazine article about education written by two parents.

6. **Sources** are given from which the information was obtained.

_____ A book about dinosaurs that includes a bibliography of 26 articles and books.

7. Use the acronym TRACKS to remember the six rules for deciding if information is believable. Now look at your ratings for the sources of information you wrote in 5-18. Change any ratings based on what you have learned.

See what you have learned about using the library to locate information:

1. What does each step in the acronym **IFES** remind you to do?

2. What are the four formats in which information in a library is packaged?

3. What is an online catalog?

4. What are the three different types of cards found in a card catalog?

5. How many main classes does the Dewey Decimal System include?

6. Why do you need call numbers?

7. What do you identify using electronic databases?

8. Why do you need more than one keyword to do a computer search?

9. What are the three Boolean connectors used in computer searches?

10. Write the word for each letter in the acronym TRACKS:

   T

   R

   A

   C

   K

   S

5-1 1. Identify sources.   2. Find sources.   3. Evaluate information.   4. Select information.

5-2 1. microform (microfilm).   2. electronic (CD ROM).   3. print (book).   4. audio visual (video cassette).   5. print (magazine).   6. microform (microfiche).

5-3 Responses will vary.

5-4 Responses will vary.

5-5 1. A man on the moon: the voyages of the Apollo astronauts.   2. Andrew Chaikin. 3. Space flight to the moon—History, Project Apollo (U.S.)—History   4. 1994. 5. Viking.   6. 670.

5-6 Responses will vary.

5-7 1. Project Apollo (U.S.), Space flight to the moon--History, Rocketry--Research--Germany --History   2. Race to the moon: America's duel with the Soviets.   3. William B. Breuer. 4. 1993.   5. Praeger.   6. 222.   7. yes.   8. 629.454

5-8 Responses will vary.

5-9 1. 500–599.   2. 900–999.   3. 600–699.   4. 400–499.   5. 000–099.   6. 200–299. 7. 100–199   8. 800–899.   9. 300–399.   10. 700–799.

5-10

751	751	751	751	751	752
.4	.422	.4225	.45	.73	

5-11 1. Articles in magazines and newspapers.   2. CD ROM databases, online databases, Internet.   3. Responses will vary.   4. A summary of an article.   5. An entire article.

5-12 1. July 20, 1969: The greatest adventure.   2. *Cobblestone: The History Magazine for Young People.*   3. Jan. 1995.   4. Pro-Quest Periodical Abstracts—Library   5. History; Space exploration; Moon.   6. Ann Keefe.   7. six pages.

5-13 1. Print index.   2. Commonly used print index.   3. *Readers' Guide* can be used to locate articles on any topic; specific subject indexes can be used to locate articles in a specific subject area.   4. Responses will vary.

5-14 title—Giant leap for mankind; first moon landing.
author—none given
magazine title—Time
illustrations—il
volume—pages 94:10–12+
month—Jl
year—'69

5-15 Responses will vary.

5-16 Responses will vary. Here is a sample response:

	1	2
Keywords	insects	plants
Other Forms of Keyword	insect	plant
Synonyms and Related Words	bug bugs bees ladybugs grasshoppers	trees shrubs bushes flowers vegetation

5-17 1.

2.

3.

5-18 Responses will vary.

5-19 Responses may vary. Recommended responses are: 1. 2; 2. 3; 3. 1; 4. 1; 5. 2; 6. 3. 7. Responses will vary but should include the information represented by TRACKS.

5-20 1. I—Identify sources.   F—Find sources.   E—Evaluate information.   S—Select information.   2. Print, electronic, audio/visual, microform.   3. A catalog where the information about each item owned by the library is stored in a computer.   4. Subject, title, author.   5. 10.   6. To locate books on library shelves.   7. Articles in magazines and newspapers.   8. To locate all the records with information on your topic.   9. and, or, not   10. T = Timely   R = Reputable   A = Accurate   C = Consistent   K = Knowledgeable   S = Sources

Using the Internet

OBJECTIVES

1. Teach students to use the Internet to find information.
2. Teach students to evaluate the information they find.

TITLES OF REPRODUCIBLE ACTIVITIES

6-1 Learning about the Internet
6-2 A Strategy for Using the Internet
6-3 Using the World Wide Web
6-4 Another Web Page
6-5 WWW Addresses to Explore
6-6 Tourist Attractions to Explore on the WWW
6-7 Schools and Libraries to Explore on the WWW
6-8 More WWW Addresses to Explore
6-9 Learning about E-Mail
6-10 Using E-Mail
6-11 Learning about FreeNets
6-12 What Makes Information Believable
6-13 Chapter Six Mastery Assessment
Answer Key

USING THE REPRODUCIBLE ACTIVITIES

After you have distributed a reproducible activity, here are suggestions for its use. Define any terms and clarify any concepts students do not know. Feel free to add further information, illustrations, or examples. Wherever possible, relate the activity to actual subject area assignments.

6-1 Learning about the Internet

The Internet is changing the way students find and use information. As schools gradually connect to the Internet, teachers are adapting their curriculum to integrate the resources offered by this new medium. In many schools, the Internet connections are located in the library. In some cases, there is also Internet access in computer labs or in the classrooms.

Two important services offered on the Internet are the World Wide Web (WWW) and e-mail:

- The WWW provides a wealth of information. However, not all of the information on the WWW is accurate. Anyone with an Internet account and a computer can create information and make it available on the WWW, which is a publishing medium with few editorial controls. The traditional filters of information, such as editors and publishers, are rarely present. Users of information found on the Internet must evaluate and select for themselves the information that is believable and useful.
- E-mail offers many opportunities for classroom instruction. Students can communicate with other students all over the world on a variety of focused topics (e.g., students from South Florida who experienced Hurricane Andrew can share their experiences with students from California who experienced flooding). Students can communicate directly with experts (e.g., a class of students studying the U.S. Civil War can ask questions of a Civil War historian), and students can send messages to public personalities (e.g., send e-mail to the president).

Review the introductory text describing the Internet. Clarify terms and concepts as necessary. Have students answer questions 1 and 2. Next, review the text about the WWW and e-mail. Have students answer questions 3 through 5.

6-2 A Strategy for Using the Internet

Use this activity to take students through the steps in a strategy for using the Internet. Use the acronym UDES to help the students remember the steps. Consider inviting the librarian to your class to discuss with students how the Internet can be used to locate information and how it compares with using other sources in the library. Then have students answer the questions on their own.

6-3 Using the World Wide Web

Information published on the WWW is located at web sites. A web site is on a computer that is connected to the Internet. The computer providing the information is called the **server**. When users are connected to the Internet, they can search for information located at web sites (on these servers). The computer used to search for the information is called the *client*.

Information on a web site is arranged in **web pages**. The top page in a set of web pages is called the **home page**. Users may jump to other pages of information located at that web site, or on another web site, by clicking on **hyperlinked** words, phrases, or images. **Navigation buttons** on a page help the user move through the pages of information at a specific web site.

Go over the introductory text with the students. Review the information on the United States Department of Energy web page. Point out that web pages vary considerably. Have students answer the questions about the web page. Encourage students to bring in examples of other web pages to share with the class.

6-4 Another Web Page

Have the students look at the web page from the National Park Service and answer the questions. Lead a discussion about how this page is different from the Department of Energy web page.

6-5 WWW Addresses to Explore

Use this activity only if your students have access to the WWW.

The Uniform Resource Locator (URL) is the address of a web site. Students can type the URL on a web browser (like Netscape Navigator, Internet Explorer, or America Online) to go directly to that web page. (The computer is actually connecting to the server and the location on the server where the information is stored.)

Have students read the introductory text about a URL. Emphasize that they must type a URL exactly as shown. Use the illustration of a sample browser to show students where a URL must be typed. Help students connect to the Internet so they can complete the activity.

6-6 Tourist Attractions to Explore on the WWW

Use this activity only if your students have access to the WWW.

Museums and tourist attractions are interesting sites to visit on the WWW. They typically have informative, well-designed web pages with many pictures. The WWW makes it possible for students to "visit" these locations.

Have students complete the activity.

6-7 Schools and Libraries to Explore on the WWW

Use this activity only if your students have access to the WWW.

Schools of all types and sizes around the world are developing their own web pages. Students can visit these schools on the WWW. Many libraries also have web pages and are interesting places to explore.

Have students complete the activity.

6-8 More WWW Addresses to Explore

Use this activity only if your students have access to the WWW.

Many web sites include a list of links to educational pages arranged by topic. These web sites are sometimes called jump sites. Each of the addresses in this activity is a jump site.

Ask students to select one of the addresses and explore the site to practice the skills they have learned. As necessary, help students connect to and search the sites they selected.

6-9 Learning about E-Mail

Use this activity to introduce students to e-mail as an Internet service. Explain that although there are many different kinds of e-mail systems (e.g., Pine, Netscape Mail, and Eudora), they all have some basic features in common. Have students read the introductory text about e-mail. Then review with them the six basic things they can do with e-mail. Have students answer the questions.

If you have e-mail in your school, demonstrate how to use it.

6-10 Using E-Mail

One of the most popular e-mail addresses is for the President of the United States. Have students compose a message to the President. If students have access to the WWW, have them send their e-mail messages.

6-11 Learning about FreeNets

FreeNets are community-based information systems about a community created by members of the community. They provide free connections to the Internet for everyone in their community. FreeNets are located in cities and towns all over the world. In many places, the public library or a consortium of local libraries creates and manages the FreeNet. They coordinate the content provided by government, businesses, organizations, and individuals. In places with FreeNets, the public library often provides training for the public. Check with your public library to see if your city or town has a FreeNet.

Review the introductory text with your students. Have them look at the choices on the sample FreeNet menu. Direct the students to complete the activity. You can vary this activity by using a menu from your own local FreeNet.

6-12 What Makes Information Believable

In 5-19, students learned the importance of evaluating the believability of information found in libraries. In this activity, they apply the same rules to evaluate information found on the WWW. The acronym TRACKS will help students remember the six rules.

Review the six rules for deciding if information is believable. Then have students complete the activity by rating the examples of information from a web page as Not Believable, Possibly Believable, or Believable.

You can extend this activity by providing information from web pages you or your students have found and having students evaluate the believability of the information based on the six rules.

6-13 Chapter Six Mastery Assessment

Have students complete this assessment at any point you believe they have learned to use the Internet. Review the results of the assessment with the students. Provide additional instruction as necessary.

The **Internet** is a worldwide network of computers and the cables that connect them. The Internet allows you to use a personal computer to connect to other computers around the world. The Internet is often called the **information superhighway** because this super network is like a road that you can travel to get to information on other computers.

1. What is the Internet?

2. Why is the Internet called the information superhighway?

The **World Wide Web** (WWW) and electronic mail (**e-mail**) are two services you can use on the Internet. You can use the WWW to find information. You can use e-mail to send messages to and receive messages from anyone around the world who has a connection to the Internet.

Refer to the graphic organizer as you answer the questions about the Internet that follow.

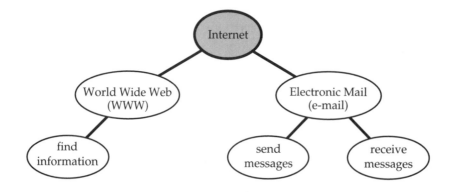

3. What two services can you use on the Internet?

4. Why would you use the World Wide Web?

5. Why would you use e-mail?

The Internet is a good place to look for information. You can use the Internet in your classroom, your library, or at home. Your teacher can tell you if the Internet is available in your school. Here are the steps that will help you remember a strategy for using the Internet.

Step One: **Use** the WWW or e-mail to find information on the Internet.

Step Two: **Determine** who created the information—governments, organizations, companies, schools, or individuals.

Step Three: **Evaluate** the believability of the source of the information.

Step Four: **Select** the information that is most believable to complete your assignment.

The acronym **UDES** will help you remember the steps in the strategy for using the Internet.

1. What does the letter **U** remind you to do?

2. The letter **D**?

3. **E**?

4. **S**?

5. Write the acronym to remember the strategy.

Information on the WWW is found on **web pages**. The first page in a set of web pages is called the **home page**. You can click on a **hyperlinked** word, phrase, or image on a web page to jump to another web page containing related information.

Look at the following web page for the United States Department of Energy. This web page contains symbols and underlined text that is hyperlinked to more information.

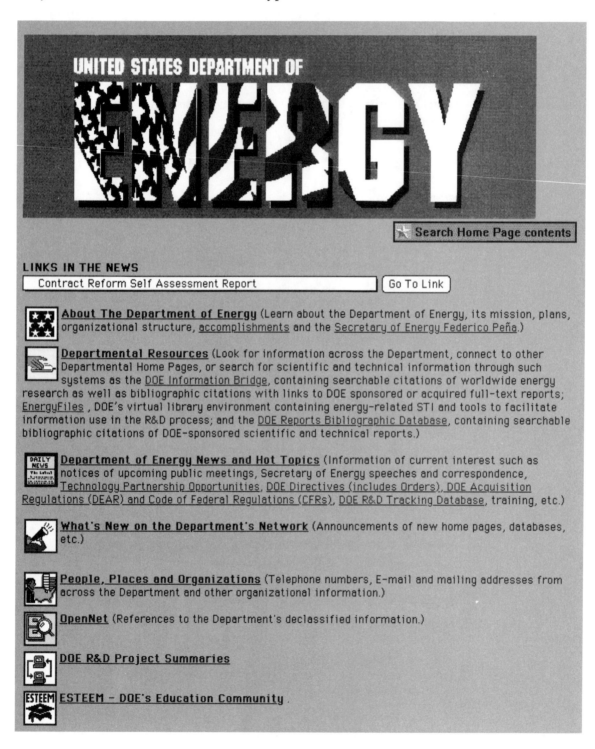

Refer to the sample web page to answer the following questions:

1. The home page usually provides information about the organization or individual who created the web page(s). What organization is responsible for the information on this home page?

2. One type of hyperlink is an image often called an **icon**. Look at the icons found on the web page. What information will you find when you click on the first icon?

   the last icon?

3. On the computer screen, **hyperlinked** words or phrases are highlighted in different colors from the rest of the text. These words or phrases are underlined when printed. *About The Department of Energy* is one of the hyperlinked phrases. What hyperlinked phrase would you select to find the telephone number of someone who works for the Department of Energy.

4. Some web pages have current information in a section called "hot topics." What is the name of the icon that links to hot topics?

Web pages are very different from one another. Some are easy to use; others are confusing. Some are useful; others are inaccurate and misleading. Some are educational; others are just for fun.

Here is another example of a web page. Look at it to answer the questions that follow.

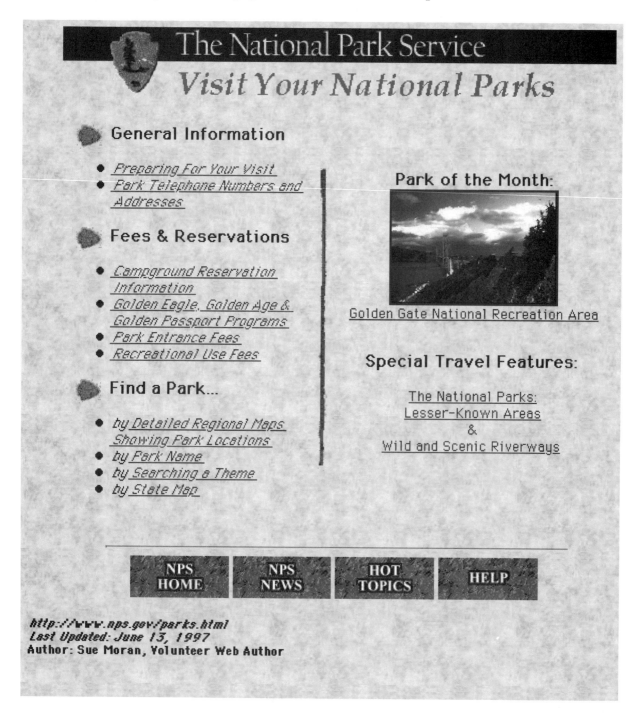

1. What is the name of the web page?

2. What organization is responsible for the information on this web page?

3. "NPS News" is one of the navigation buttons on the page. Write the name of the navigation button you would click on to go to the home page.

4. "Find a Park by Park Name" is the hyperlinked phrase you would select to jump to a web page about Yosemite National Park. Which hyperlinked phrase would you select to find the names of national parks in California?

5. Which hyperlinked phrase would you select to find out how much it costs to use the recreational facilities of Yosemite National Park?

6. The bottom of a web page often provides information about the page itself, such as who created it, when it was last updated, and e-mail addresses. On what date was the information on this page updated?

An address on the WWW is called the **URL (Uniform Resource Locator)**. If you know the URL for a web page, you can type it in a web browser to go to that web page. After you press the ENTER key, the Internet will connect your computer with the computer where the information for that web page is located. Look at the sample screen for a web browser to see where the URL is typed.

File	Edit	View	Go	Bookmarks	Options	Window	Help
Back	Forward	Home	Reload	Open	Print	Find	Stop

Type URL
→
(Go to:
or
Location)

Go to: [   ]

Text only

FIU
LIBRARIES

**Welcome to the
Florida International
University Libraries**

North Campus – University Park

ru OCLC FirstSearch. Select FirstSearch under Electronic Library menu.

You must type the URL *exactly* as you see it! Follow these rules.

❏ Type upper case and lower case letters exactly as given.

❏ Include _ or / or ~ or . or % or - exactly as given.

❏ Do not add any extra spaces or dots (periods).

1. Type the following URL

   http://www.mindspring.com/~zoonet/www_virtual_lib/zoos.html

Write the name of the web page you found at this address.

2. Type the following URL

   http://duke.usask.ca/%7Escottp/free.html

Write the name of the web page you found at this address.

Here is a list of tourist attractions, museums, and other places you might like to visit. Visit one or more of these places.

Metropolitan Museum of Art

http://www.metmuseum.org

NASA/Kennedy Space Station

http://www.ksc.nasa.gov/ksc.html

Louvre

http://www.paris.org/Musees/Louvre/

National Baseball Hall of Fame and Museum

http://www.baseballhalloffame.org/index.html

Smithsonian Museum

http://www.si.edu

San Diego Zoo

http://www.sandiegozoo.org/Zoo/zoo.html

Write a newspaper headline that tells something special about the place you visited on the WWW. Then write a sentence or two explaining what someone would find when they visit that place.

Schools and Libraries to Explore on the WWW

Here is a list of schools and libraries that you can explore on the WWW. Each of these URLs lists many schools or libraries to visit. Select one URL. Then select one school or library listed on that URL to visit.

K-12 Schools on the WWW

http://web66.coled.umn.edu/schools.html

U.S. Universities and Community Colleges on the WWW

http://www.utexas.edu/world/univ/

School Libraries on the Web

http://www.cusd.chico.k12.ca.us/~pmilbury/slib.html

Public Libraries on the Web

http://sunsite.Berkeley.EDU/Libweb/usa-pub

Academic Libraries on the WWW

http://sunsite.Berkeley.EDU/Libweb/usa-acad.html

Draw a picture that shows the most interesting thing you learned when you "visited" a school or library on the WWW.

Here are some addresses to explore on the WWW. Each of these URLs lists many topics to select. Select one URL. Then select one topic listed on that URL to explore.

CyberBee

http://www.cyberbee.com

Classroom Connect by Subject

http://www2.classroom.net/databases/grades/edufind.html

Yahooligans

http://www.yahooligans.com/text

Fifty Extraordinary Experiences for Internet Kids

http://www.well.com/user/polly/ikyp.exp.html

David Levin's Learning@Web.Sites

http://www.ecnet.net/users/gdlevin/home.html

You can use **e-mail** (electronic mail) to send messages to and receive messages from anyone around the world who has a connection to the Internet. You must turn on your computer to send an e-mail message. However, you can receive e-mail in your mailbox even when your computer is turned off.

When you turn on your computer and open your mailbox, you will find any new messages that have been sent to you. There are many different e-mail systems that you can use. They may look very different from one another, but they all provide the same type of service. Here are six things you can do with e-mail.

Send—send a message

Read—read a message

Delete—erase a message

Forward—send a message to another mailbox

Reply—answer the person who wrote you the message

Print—print a message

1. What is the purpose of e-mail?

2. To whom can you send e-mail?

3. Can you send e-mail when your computer is turned off?

4. Can you receive e-mail when your computer is turned off?

5. What are six things you can do with e-mail messages?

You can also use e-mail to send messages to famous people. Here is the URL to send e-mail to the President of the United States.

http://www.whitehouse.gov/WH/Mail/html/Mail_President.html

What would you like to say to the President in an e-mail message? Write your message here:

Use what you know about e-mail to send your message to the President.

A **FreeNet** is a computer information system for your town or city. There are FreeNets throughout the United States and all over the world. FreeNets provide a free connection to the Internet. This connection may allow you to send and receive e-mail and to search for information on the WWW. In many cases, however, you will not be able to view the pictures that go with the information on the web page.

Here is a sample FreeNet page from the WWW:

SEFLIN Free-Net
Southeast Florida Library Information Network, Inc.

[Free-Net Registration & User Information | New Items & Training]
[Adding Your Information | Make SEFLIN Free-Net Your Home Page]

Arts & Entertainment	Business, Money & Taxes
Education & Schools	Government & Communities
Home, Garden & Daily Living	Legal, Crime & Safety
Libraries & Literature	Medicine & Health
News and Media Resources	Religion & Philosophy
Science & Technology	Social Services
Special Interest Groups	Sports, Recreation & Travel
Youth - Kids & Teens	Other Free-Nets & Beyond

The SEFLIN Free-Net is sponsored, operated, and governed by the Southeast Florida Library Information Network [SEFLIN], a non-profit organization of libraries in Broward, Dade, Palm Beach, Martin & Monroe counties.

THANKS! to our community [Sponsors & Supporters] for their support in making the Free-Net truly a community resource 'By the People -- For the People'.

Index & Internet Search Tools | HELP

SEFLIN Menu = ([   ]) [Now]

Thanks to SEFLIN Free-Net Supporter: *Martin County Public Library System*

Refer to the sample FreeNet page. Write the hyperlinked phrase you would select to do each of the following:

   1. Find out what your mayor is planning.

   2. Get the home schedule for a local sports team.

   3. Find information for a science fair.

   4. Find out about local crime watch groups.

   5. Connect to library online catalogs.

   6. Find out what films are showing in your town or city

   7. Connect to a FreeNet in another city.

Use the acronym **TRACKS** to remember six rules for deciding if information is believable. The acronym TRACKS stands for:

    Timely   Reputable   Accurate   Consistent   Knowledgeable   Sources

Read each rule for deciding if information from a web page is believable. Then read the information from a web page. Write 1, 2, or 3 to show how believable the information is based upon the rule.

    1   Not Believable
    2   Possibly Believable
    3   Believable

1. The information is **Timely**.

   _____ Information about the Peace Treaty in Northern Ireland was found on a web page last updated on 12-4-96.

2. The information is from a **Reputable** source.

   _____ Information about life on Mars is from one of the NASA web pages.

3. The information is **Accurate**.

   _____ Statistics about population is from a government web page maintained by the U.S. Department of the Census.

4. The information is **Consistent** with what other experts say about the topic.

   _____ Information on the web page says that the earth is the closest planet to the sun.

5. The information is written by one or more persons **Knowledgeable** in the field.

   _____ The information about the solar system is from a web page created by an 8th grader.

6. **Sources** are given from which the information was obtained.

   _____ The web page about smoking provides references to cancer research in articles and books.

See what you have learned about using the Internet to find information:

1. What are two services you can use on the Internet?

2. What does each letter in the acronym UDES remind you to do?

3. What is a home page?

4. What is a URL?

5. What Internet service can be used to send and receive messages?

6. What free computer information system can you use to get information about your town or city?

7. Write the word for each letter in the acronym TRACKS.

T

R

A

C

K

S

6-1 1. Worldwide network of computers and the cables that connect them. 2. Because it is like a road that you can travel to get to information on other computers. 3. World Wide Web (WWW) and Electronic Mail (e-mail). 4. To find information. 5. To send messages to and receive messages from anyone around the world who has a connection to the Internet.

6-2 1. Use the WWW or e-mail to find information on the Internet. 2. Determine who created the information. 3. Evaluate the believability of the source of the information. 4. Select the information that is most believable to complete your assignment.

6-3 1. United States Department of Energy. 2. Information about the Department of Energy; information about ESTEEM—DOE'S Education Community. 3. People, Places, and Organizations. 4. Daily News.

6-4 1. Visit Your National Parks. 2. The National Park Service. 3. NPS HOME. 4. *Find a Park by State Map*. 5. *Recreational Use Fees*. 6. June 13, 1997.

6-5 1. WWW Virtual Library: Zoos. 2. FreeNets and Community Networks.

6-6 Responses will vary.

6-7 Responses will vary.

6-8 No written response required.

6-9 1. To send and receive messages on the Internet. 2. Anyone who has a connection to the Internet. 3. No. 4. Yes. 5. Send, Read, Delete, Forward, Reply, Print.

6-10 Responses will vary.

6-11 1. Government and Communities. 2. Sports, Recreation & Travel. 3. Science & Technology. 4. Legal, Crime & Safety. 5. Libraries & Literature. 6. Arts & Entertainment. 7. Other Free-Nets and Beyond.

6-12 Responses will vary. Recommended responses are: 1. 2; 2. 3; 3. 3; 4. 1; 5. 2; 6. 3.

6-13 1. World Wide Web (WWW) and electronic mail (e-mail). 2. Use the WWW or e-mail to find information on the Internet. Determine who created the information. Evaluate the believability of the creator of the information. Select the information that is most valid to complete your assignment. 3. The first page in a set of web pages. 4. A URL is an address on the WWW. 5. E-mail. 6. FreeNet. 7. T = Timely R = Reputable A = Accurate C = Consistent K = Knowledgeable S = Sources.

CHAPTER SEVEN

Using Reference Sources

OBJECTIVES

1. Teach students about reference sources available in both print and electronic formats.
2. Teach students how to locate and use basic reference sources.

TITLES OF REPRODUCIBLE ACTIVITIES

7-1 Learning about Types of Reference Sources
7-2 Learning about Electronic Reference Sources
7-3 Learning about Dictionaries
7-4 Using a Dictionary
7-5 Using Different Dictionaries
7-6 Using a Thesaurus
7-7 Learning about Encyclopedias
7-8 Learning about Electronic Encyclopedias
7-9 Locating Print and Electronic Encyclopedias
7-10 Using a Print Encyclopedia
7-11 Using a Multimedia Encyclopedia
7-12 Using an Almanac
7-13 Using an Atlas
7-14 Using an Electronic Atlas
7-15 Finding Biographical Information
7-16 Chapter Seven Mastery Assessment
Answer Key

USING THE REPRODUCIBLE ACTIVITIES

After you have distributed a reproducible activity, here are suggestions for its use. Define any terms and clarify any concepts students do not know. Feel free to add further information, illustrations, or examples. Wherever possible, relate the activity to actual subject-area assignments.

7-1 Learning about Types of Reference Sources

Traditional reference sources owned by libraries in print formats are among the most authoritative sources for factual information. Most have a reputation for using experts to compile and write the information provided, and their standards for quality control are usually rigorous. The most frequently used types of reference sources are dictionaries, encyclopedias, thesauruses, almanacs, atlases, and biographical sources. Activities are included in this chapter for each of these sources.

Use the graphic organizer and text to acquaint students with frequently used types of reference sources. Show examples of these types of reference sources. Have students answer the questions. Ask students to share what they wrote about their experiences using reference sources.

7-2 Learning about Electronic Reference Sources

Increasingly, many publishers of traditional print reference sources are publishing their products in electronic formats, including CD ROM and on the Internet via the WWW. In many cases, the electronic versions offer additional features, such as the ability to search by keywords using Boolean connectors; hyperlinked words, phrases, and images to click on and jump to related information; and multimedia applications such as audio, video, and animation. Some electronic versions of reference sources are text-only without any multimedia features. Usually the text of the electronic version is the same as the print version.

Using electronic reference sources requires basic computer skills such as: keyboard/mouse skills; the ability to select and use keywords and Boolean connectors; and some familiarity with tool/task bars, pop-up windows, scrolling, and navigating. Furthermore, schools must have the resources to provide access to electronic reference sources on computers for students.

Use the graphic organizer and text to acquaint students with the formats for electronic reference sources. Have students complete the activity. Ask students to share what they wrote about their experiences using electronic reference sources.

7-3 Learning about Dictionaries

Use the Venn diagram graphic organizer and text to acquaint students with abridged and unabridged dictionaries. Show students examples of each type. Have students answer the questions.

7-4 Using a Dictionary

Have students read about the different types of information found on a dictionary page. Explain any terms they do not understand. Point out that there may be variations between dictionaries but that the basic information remains the same. Then have students complete the activity.

7-5 Using Different Dictionaries

Use this activity to have students look for and use different kinds of dictionaries at home and in the library. Tell students that they may need to use more than one dictionary to find information about a word. Then have them look up the meaning of the word *joculator*. This fairly obscure word was chosen so that students will have to use more than one dictionary. You may provide additional words, but be sure that they are words *not* included in some dictionaries. Have students answer the questions.

7-6 Using a Thesaurus

Review the introductory text with students. Show the students any thesauruses that may be available. Have students use a thesaurus to find synonyms for the words. Point out that they must pay attention to the form of the word listed (e.g., noun, verb).

7-7 Learning about Encyclopedias

Encyclopedias make up a large part of a library's reference collection. They are known for their accuracy, expertise, and currency. Encyclopedias vary in the features they provide. There are four main types of encyclopedias: general, single volume, children and young adult, and subject encyclopedias. For each type, many different titles are available, published by different publishers. For example, some encyclopedias for children and young adults are: the *World Book Encyclopedia, Compton's Encyclopedia, Grolier's New Book of Knowledge,* the *Oxford Children's Encyclopedia,* and the *Children's Britannica.*

Review the introductory text with students. Have students read about the four types of encyclopedias. Then have them write what is contained in each.

7-8 Learning about Electronic Encyclopedias

Many publishers now sell their encyclopedias in both print and electronic formats. The electronic version may be on CD ROM, as are the multimedia encyclopedias frequently sold with new computers, or it may be available on the Internet. Sometimes the electronic version of an encyclopedia is multimedia and sometimes it is text only.

Another possibility is that the electronic encyclopedia is made available on a network. For example, in the state of Florida, the *Encyclopedia Britannica* is available in school and public libraries throughout the state.

Review the differences between print and multimedia encyclopedias. Then have students complete the activity. To answer questions 5 and 6, students will need to apply what they learned in previous activities. Have students share their responses to these two questions.

7-9 Locating Print and Electronic Encyclopedias

Have students complete the activity. Remind students to ask the librarian for assistance if they cannot find one or more of the types of encyclopedias.

7-10 Using a Print Encyclopedia

Tell students that they should always use the index of an encyclopedia because they may not find information about a topic in the volume in which they expect it to be. For example, a student looking for information about *cars* might go to the "C" volume but may not find an entry for *cars*. However, if the student looks for *cars* in the index volume, the entry for *cars* may provide a cross-reference to the "A" volume for *automobiles*, or the T volume for *transportation*.

Demonstrate how a keyword and index can be used to locate information about a topic in a print encyclopedia. Use the sample index entry to explain the types of information found in an encyclopedia index entry. Then have students look at the sample entry for "Moon" and answer the questions.

7-11 Using a Multimedia Encyclopedia

Use this activity only if the students have access to a multimedia encyclopedia.

Multimedia encyclopedias on CD ROM are very common and may be included with the purchase of a new computer. Using a multimedia encyclopedia successfully require basic computer skills: keyboard/mouse skills, scrolling, using navigation buttons, and some familiarity with tool/task bars and pop-up windows.

Multimedia encyclopedias use many icons to help identify the different media included in an article. The icon used may vary with the product, but the media identified are the same. For example, an icon for a map may be a globe in one product but a compass in another.

Have students read the introductory text about icons. Go over each of the examples with students. Then have them use a multimedia encyclopedia to find information about Haiti. For each icon, have them write what happened when they clicked on the icon, and what they learned about Haiti.

Depending on the multimedia encyclopedia used by the students, not all icons may be found. You may substitute another country or provide more countries from which students can choose.

7-12 Using an Almanac

Review the introductory text with students. Then tell them to use the index to find facts in an almanac. Caution students that, depending on the almanac they use, the index may be in the front, middle, or back. Have students locate almanacs in the library to complete the activity. Tell them to use the current edition. You can use this activity as a group project or as a competition between individuals and/or groups. Later, have students share their experiences in using almanacs to locate facts.

7-13 Using an Atlas

As with encyclopedias, there are different types of atlases. A general world atlas contains maps showing physical and political features of countries throughout the world. Most general world atlases include sections of maps on specific topics, such as climate, population, or health. A historical atlas contains maps that portray an event or show how something developed or changed over a period of time. Historical atlases include information about topics such as changes in borders, military campaigns, exploration, or culture. A subject atlas contains maps related to a specific place or topic. Atlases are available in both print and electronic formats.

Review the introductory text with students. Emphasize that students may have to use more than one type of atlas to answer the questions. Help students locate atlases to complete the activity. You can use this activity as a group project or as a competition between individuals and/or groups. Later, have students share their experiences in using atlases to locate information.

7-14 Using an Electronic Atlas

Use this activity only if your students have access to an electronic atlas or to the WWW.

Many atlases are published in both print and electronic formats. The electronic version may be on CD ROM, as are the multimedia atlases sometimes included with new computers, or it may be available on the Internet, as is the atlas available on the WWW at the National Geographic web site. Find out if your library has an electronic atlas.

Review the introductory text with students. Then have them use an electronic atlas to find information about Sudan. Have students answer the questions about the information they found. Then lead a discussion about the differences between print and multimedia atlases. Ask students to share their experiences using an electronic atlas.

7-15 Finding Biographical Information

Biographical reference sources provide information about famous people, living or dead. Some biographical sources provide information about authors only. Students can often find information about more people in these sources than in any other sources.

Biographical sources are also published in both print and electronic format. Electronic biographical sources are available on CD ROM as well as on the WWW.

Review the words *biography* and *autobiography* with students. Tell them that they may find information about a person in an encyclopedia, but that biographical sources often provide more information than encyclopedias. Also point out that biographical sources contain information about people who do not appear in encyclopedias. Then have students locate information about each person listed using biographical sources in your library.

7-16 Chapter Seven Mastery Assessment

Have students complete this assessment at any point you believe they have learned about reference sources and how and when to use them. Review the results of the assessment with the students. Provide additional instruction as necessary.

Reference sources are used to find background information on a topic, to find facts, and to get a quick answer to a question. Look at the graphic organizer for types of reference sources. Then read about it.

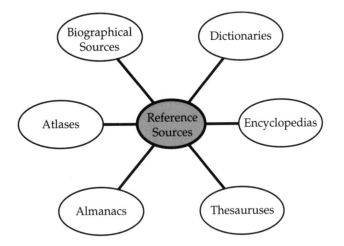

The most frequently used types of reference sources are dictionaries, encyclopedias, thesauruses, almanacs, atlases, and biographical sources. Reference sources are usually shelved in their own section of the library. Ask the librarian to help you locate reference sources.

1. What are three uses of reference sources?

2. What are the six most frequently used types of reference sources?

3. Who can help you locate reference sources?

4. What reference sources have you used in the past?

Look at the graphic organizer for electronic reference sources. Then read about it.

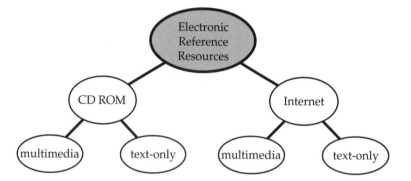

Many reference sources are available in electronic formats. The graphic organizer shows that the two most common electronic formats are CD ROM and the Internet.

The graphic organizer also shows that the CD ROM is available in both multimedia and text-only formats. The Internet also offers both multimedia and text-only formats.

Multimedia formats contain images, sound, video, and/or animation in addition to text. Text-only formats contain text but do not include images, sound, video, and animation.

1. In what two electronic formats are reference sources available?

2. What do multimedia reference sources contain?

3. What are text-only CD ROM reference sources?

4. What electronic reference sources have you used in the past?

Look at the graphic organizer for dictionaries. Then read about it.

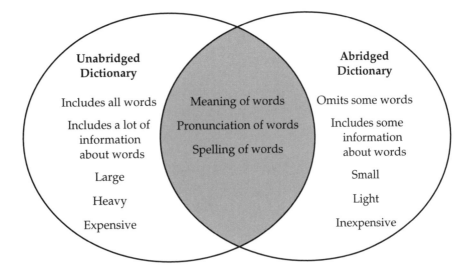

Dictionaries are reference books that provide information about the meaning, pronunciation, and spelling of words. Two important types of dictionaries you should know about are unabridged dictionaries and abridged dictionaries.

Unabridged Dictionaries

Unabridged dictionaries attempt to include all words currently in use in a language. Because they include all the words and a lot of information about the words, unabridged dictionaries are very large and heavy. They usually are expensive. An example of an unabridged dictionary is the *Random House Dictionary of the English Language*.

Abridged Dictionaries

Abridged dictionaries include only the words most frequently used in a language. Because they include fewer words and less information about the words, they are smaller, lighter and less expensive than unabridged dictionaries. An example of an abridged dictionary is the *American Heritage Dictionary*.

1. What information do dictionaries provide?

2. What type of dictionary includes almost every word that people use today?

3. How is an abridged dictionary different from an unabridged dictionary?

4. What type of dictionary is smaller, lighter, and less expensive?

Read about the types of information you will find on a dictionary page. Refer to this information to complete the activity.

1. **Guide words:** There are two guide words at the top of every page in a dictionary. The first guide word is called the *opening guide word*. It shows the first word on the page. The second guide word is called the *closing guide word*. It shows the last word on the page.

2. **Entry words:** Entry words are the words listed and defined on the page. They are in bold type to make them easy to locate.

3. **Phonetic respellings:** Each entry word is followed by a phonetic respelling, usually in parentheses. The respelling uses symbols and letters to show you how to pronounce the word.

4. **Part of Speech:** After the respelling you usually will find an abbreviation that tells the part of speech for the entry word. The abbreviation is often in italics. Here are the abbreviations you will find for the common parts of speech:

   n = noun   *v* = verb   *adj* = adjective
   pron = pronoun   *adv* = adverb   *prep* = preposition

5. **Definitions:** The definitions for each entry word are included. They are numbered to show how commonly they are used. The most common definition is listed as **1.** The next most common definition follows as **2,** and so on.

6. **Variants of the Word:** The entry word may also include different forms of the word. For example, *directed, directing,* and *directs* may be included with the entry word *direct.*

7. **Origin or etymology:** Some dictionaries include information telling the language from which the word came. Sometimes this information is in brackets [   ]. In some cases, an abbreviation for the original language may be included, such as G for Greek or L for Latin.

8. **Usage:** In some cases, a sentence containing the entry word is provided to show how the word might be used.

9. **Synonym or antonym:** Sometimes a synonym and/or an antonym for the entry word is provided. The abbreviation *syn* is used for synonyms, and *ant* is used for antonyms.

10. **Illustration:** Sometimes drawings or photographs are included to illustrate the word.

11. **Short and long pronunciation keys:** The *short pronunciation key* is usually found at the bottom of the right-hand dictionary page. It contains letters, symbols, and words that will help you pronounce words correctly. If the short pronunciation key does not help you pronounce an entry word, then look at the *long pronunciation key* found at the front of your dictionary. These pronunciation keys can be used to help you understand the phonetic respellings.

Here is a sample entry from a dictionary. In each box, place the number for its description.

☐
glitter

☐
gloss

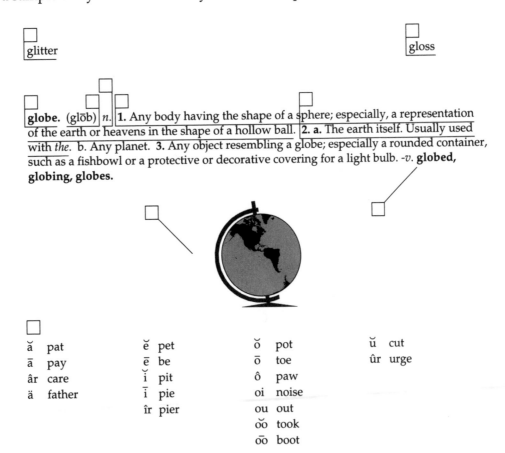

☐ ☐ ☐ ☐
globe. (glōb) *n.* **1.** Any body having the shape of a sphere; especially, a representation of the earth or heavens in the shape of a hollow ball. **2. a.** The earth itself. Usually used with *the.* b. Any planet. **3.** Any object resembling a globe; especially a rounded container, such as a fishbowl or a protective or decorative covering for a light bulb. *-v.* **globed, globing, globes.**

☐

ă pat	ĕ pet	ŏ pot	ŭ cut
ā pay	ē be	ō toe	ûr urge
âr care	ĭ pit	ô paw	
ä father	ī pie	oi noise	
	îr pier	ou out	
		ŏŏ took	
		ōō boot	

If you cannot find your word in one dictionary, try another. You may need to use a larger, unabridged dictionary to find your word.

Look up the following word: **joculator**

Answer the questions:

1. What is the most common definition for joculator?

2. What is the title of the dictionary in which you found this word?

3. Is this an abridged or unabridged dictionary?

4. In how many dictionaries did you look before you found this word?

A **thesaurus** is a reference source that contains synonyms for commonly used words. A **synonym** is a word having the same or nearly the same meaning as another word. Words in a thesaurus are listed in alphabetical order. Following each word is its part of speech and a list of synonyms. You use a thesaurus to select words that will help you express an idea precisely.

Use a thesaurus to find synonyms for the following words. Write all the synonyms you find.

1. grab

2. command

3. hurricane

4. struggle (*n*)

5. tired

6. mild

7. crowd (*v*)

An **encyclopedia** contains articles on a variety of subjects written by experts. The articles are arranged in alphabetical order by topic. There are four types of encyclopedias with which you should be familiar:

1. **General encyclopedias** include overview articles on a wide range of topics. The articles are arranged alphabetically in a set of volumes. Illustrations are also included. The last volume in the set is the index. Information is kept up-to-date with articles published in yearbooks or supplements. An example of a general encyclopedia is the *Encyclopedia Americana*.

2. **Single-volume encyclopedias** include short articles arranged in alphabetical order. There is no index or table of contents. An example of a single-volume encyclopedia is the *Random House Encyclopedia*.

3. **Encyclopedias for children and young adults** are general encyclopedias written for a specific age group. The articles include many illustrations and study aids and are easier to read than articles in other encyclopedias. An example of an encyclopedia for children and young adults is the *World Book Encyclopedia*.

4. **Subject encyclopedias** are found for many subjects, such as geography, science, and art. Some are written for adults, others for younger students. Articles in a subject encyclopedia are longer and more technical than those found in general encyclopedias. An example of a subject encyclopedia is *Dorling Kindersley's Science Encyclopedia*.

What is contained in each of the following?

1. General encyclopedias:

2. Single-volume encyclopedias:

3. Encyclopedias for children and young adults:

4. Subject encyclopedias:

Electronic encyclopedias are used with a computer. Two formats for electronic encyclopedias are CD ROM and the Internet.

Encyclopedias on CD ROM may be multimedia or text-only. Multimedia encyclopedias include images, sound, video, and/or either animation as well as text. Text-only electronic encyclopedias do not include pictures or any other media.

Encyclopedias on the Internet also may be either multimedia or text-only. Multimedia encyclopedias on CD ROM are the most popular format of electronic encyclopedia. An example of a multimedia encyclopedia on CD ROM is *Microsoft Encarta 96 Encyclopedia.*

1. What are two formats of electronic encyclopedias?

2. What does a multimedia encyclopedia include that a text-only encyclopedia does not?

3. What is the most popular format of electronic encyclopedia?

4. Describe an experience you have had using an electronic encyclopedia.

5. What do you think are some advantages of using a multimedia encyclopedia instead of a print encyclopedia?

6. What do you think are some advantages of using a print encyclopedia instead of a multimedia encyclopedia?

Locating Print and Electronic Encyclopedias

Find an example of each of the following types of encyclopedias. Write its title and call number. Then ✔ **Print** or **Electronic** to show the format of the encyclopedia that you found.

General Encyclopedia

Title

Call number

Print _____   Electronic _____

Encyclopedia for Children and Young Adults

Title

Call number

Print _____   Electronic _____

Subject Encyclopedia

Title

Call number

Print _____   Electronic _____

Single-Volume Encyclopedia

Title

Call number

Print _____   Electronic _____

To look for information in an encyclopedia, begin by selecting the most important word in your topic. This word is your **keyword**. Look for your keyword in the index to the encyclopedia. The index is usually the last volume. Select another word in your topic if you cannot find your first keyword in the index.

Using the keyword *moon* from the topic "Space exploration and the moon," you might find the following index entry. Study this sample index entry and answer the questions.

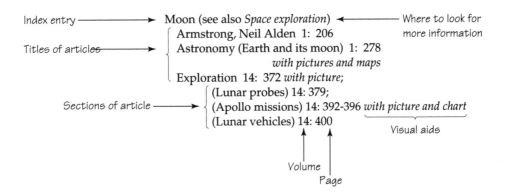

1. What is the index entry?

2. Where would you look for more information about the index entry?

3. What are the titles of the articles for the index entry?

4. In the article "Armstrong, Neil Alden 1: 206," what does "1" stand for?

5. In the article "Armstrong, Neil Alden 1: 206," what does the "206" stand for?

Using a Multimedia Encyclopedia 7-11

Icons are used to find information in a multimedia encyclopedia. An **icon** is a hyperlinked image used in a computer database. Here are some common icons you might find when using a multimedia encyclopedia. Look at each icon to learn what it stands for and what happens when you click on it.

Icon	What it stands for:	What happens when you click on it:
	Video	Videoclip appears. *Example:* Scenes of hurricanes and the destruction they cause.
	Sound	Sound occurs. *Examples:* Alligator growl; rap group performing; audio broadcast of astronaut when man first landed on the moon.
	Animation	Movement occurs. *Example:* Diagram of how a rocket works showing various stages and narrated with an explanation of each step in the process.
	Picture	Picture appears. *Examples:* Photograph of a platypus, famous athlete, movie star.
	Map	Map appears. *Example:* Map of the Middle East with names of places hyperlinked.
	Table/chart/graph	Table, chart, or graph appears. *Example:* Chart showing endangered plants and animals, graph showing world population, table showing characteristics of the moon.

134
Copyright © 1998 by Allyn and Bacon

Use a multimedia encyclopedia to look up the country *Haiti*. Find each of the following icons or the icon used by that encyclopedia for that function. Click on each. Write what happened. Then write a statement that tells what you learned.

1.

What happened when I clicked on it:

What I learned about Haiti:

2.

What happened when I clicked on it:

What I learned about Haiti:

3.

What happened when I clicked on it:

What I learned about Haiti:

4.

What happened when I clicked on it:

What I learned about Haiti:

5.

What happened when I clicked on it:

What I learned about Haiti:

6.

What happened when I clicked on it:

What I learned about Haiti:

An **almanac** is a single-volume reference book containing facts on a wide range of topics. Almanacs are revised each year so that the facts they contain are current. Some frequently used almanacs are the following:

Information Please Almanac
New York Public Library Desk Reference
World Almanac and Book of Facts

Use the current edition of one of these almanacs or any other almanac to answer the questions that follow. You may need to look in more than one almanac. Write the title of the almanac containing the facts needed to answer the question and the page number(s) on which the facts were found.

1. What is the name of the largest nuclear power plant in the United States?

   Answer:

   Title of Almanac:

   Page(s):

2. What was the population of the United States in 1990?

   Answer:

   Title of Almanac:

   Page(s):

3. What language is spoken by the most people in the world?

   Answer:

   Title of Almanac:

   Page(s):

An **atlas** is a collection of maps. There are many different types of atlases. Two common atlases are the following:

> *Hammond Atlas of the World*
> *Times Atlas of World History*

Go to your library and find the atlases available there. Write the names of at least two here.

Use an atlas to answer the questions that follow. You may need to use more than one atlas. Write the title of the atlas containing the information needed to answer the question and the page number(s) on which the information was found.

1. What are the names of the countries that border Libya on the continent of Africa?

   Answer:

   Title of Atlas:

   Page(s):

2. What is the name of the mountain range in Russia that is east of Moscow?

   Answer:

   Title of Atlas:

   Page(s):

3. Find a map that shows the average rainfall of Puerto Rico. How many inches of rain fall in Puerto Rico in one year?

   Answer:

   Title of Atlas:

   Page(s):

Atlases can be found in electronic formats. They are on CD ROM and on the Internet. Some atlases on CD ROM or on the Internet are multimedia.

Some popular atlases on CD ROM are the following:

> Encarta 97 World Atlas
> 3D Atlas
> National Geographic Picture Atlas of the World

National Geographic Society also has a free *Map Machine Atlas* on the WWW at:

> http://www.nationalgeographic.com/resources/ngo/maps/index.html

Use an electronic atlas to look up the country *Sudan*. Use the atlas to answer these questions.

1. Did you find a political map of Sudan?

2. Did you find a physical map of Sudan?

3. What other maps did you find for Sudan?

4. Can you find a map of Sudan by typing in the name of the country?

5. Can you *zoom in* on a region in Sudan?

6. Did you find an article about Sudan?

7. Did you find any photographs?

8. What did you like best about using the electronic atlas?

Biographical sources are reference books that provide information about the lives and accomplishments of famous people, living or dead. The entries vary in length from one paragraph to several pages. Biographical sources include information about people about whom no biography or autobiography exists.

Some common biographical sources are the following:

Something about the Author   *Webster's Biographical Dictionary*
Dictionary of Scientific Biography   *Grolier Library of North American Biographies*

Biographical sources are also available in electronic format. Two common biographical sources are the following:

U • X • L Biographies
Junior DISCovering Authors

Use one of these biographical sources or any other biographical source in your library to find information about the famous people that follow. Next to each name, write the title of the biographical source containing information about that person. Also write the page number(s) where the information appears. If there is a volume number, write that, too.

	Title of Biographical Source	*Volume/Page(s)*
Harriet Tubman		
Jackie Robinson		
John Glenn		
Louisa May Alcott		
Cesar Chavez		

See what you have learned about using reference sources.

1. What are the six most frequently used types of reference sources?

2. What is the difference between multimedia and text-only reference sources?

3. What is an abridged dictionary?

4. What is a thesaurus?

5. What are four types of encyclopedias?

6. What are two formats for electronic encyclopedias?

7. What information does the index entry for an encyclopedia provide?

8. What is an icon?

9. What is an almanac?

10. What is an atlas?

11. What are biographical sources?

7-1 1. To find background information on a topic, to find facts, and to get a quick answer to a question.   2. Dictionaries, encyclopedias, thesauruses, almanacs, atlases, and biographical sources.   3. Librarian.   4. Responses will vary.

7-2 1. CD ROM; Internet.   2. Images, sound, video, animation, and/or text.   3. Reference sources that contain text but do not contain images, sound, video, or animation.   4. Responses will vary.

7-3 1. Information about the meaning, pronunciation, and spelling of words.   2. Unabridged. 3. Omits words that are not frequently used; contains less information about words; is smaller, lighter, and less expensive.   4. Abridged.

7-4

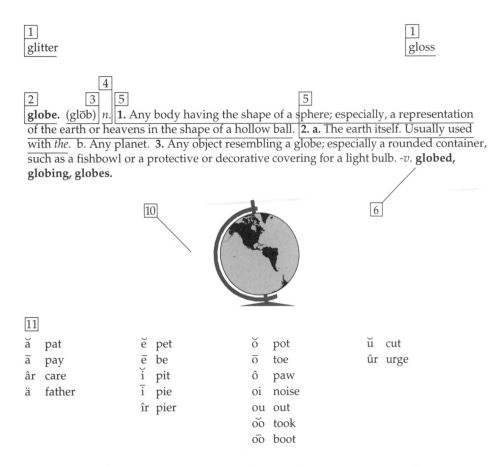

```
 1                                                       1
 glitter                                                 gloss
```

```
              4
 2        3   5
 globe.  (glōb) n.  1. Any body having the shape of a sphere; especially, a representation
 of the earth or heavens in the shape of a hollow ball. 2. a. The earth itself. Usually used
 with the. b. Any planet. 3. Any object resembling a globe; especially a rounded container,
 such as a fishbowl or a protective or decorative covering for a light bulb. -v. globed,
 globing, globes.
```

```
 11
 ă    pat          ĕ    pet          ŏ    pot          ŭ    cut
 ā    pay          ē    be           ō    toe          ûr   urge
 âr   care         ĭ    pit          ô    paw
 ä    father       ī    pie          oi   noise
                   îr   pier         ou   out
                                     o͝o   took
                                     o͞o   boot
```

7-5 1. The first definition of *joculator* is: "a professional jester, a person who amuses others." 2. Responses will vary.   3. Responses will vary.   4. Responses will vary.

7-6 Responses will vary.

7-7 1. Overview articles on a wide range of topics.   2. Short articles arranged in alphabetical order.   3. Articles that include many illustrations and study aids and that are easier to read than articles in other encyclopedias.   4. Long and technical articles.

7-8 1. CD ROM; Internet.   2. Images, sound, video, and/or animation.   3. Multimedia encyclopedias on CD ROM.   4. Responses will vary.   5. Responses will vary but may include: "Can combine keywords to search for topics"; "Can see images and videos and hear sounds, more fun."   6. Responses will vary but may include: "More people can use it at once"; "Don't need a computer"; "Don't need to know how to use a computer."

7-9 Responses will vary.

7-10 1. Moon. 2. Space exploration. 3. Armstrong, Neil Alden; Astronomy (Earth and its moon); Exploration. 4. Volume. 5. Page.

7-11 1. Movement occurs; information about Haiti will vary. 2. Sound occurs; information about Haiti will vary. 3. Map appears; information about Haiti will vary. 4. Table/chart/graph appears; information about Haiti will vary. 5. Picture appears; information about Haiti will vary. 6. Videoclip appears; information about Haiti will vary.

7-12 1. Houston Power and Light. 2. 248,709,873. 3. Mandarin. (Titles and pages will vary with almanac used.)

7-13 1. Algeria; Tunisia; Egypt; Sudan; Chad; Niger. 2. Ural Mountains. 3. 59 inches.

7-14 Responses will vary depending on the electronic atlas used.

7-15 Responses will vary.

7-16 1. Dictionaries, encyclopedias, thesauruses, almanacs, atlases, and biographical sources. 2. Multimedia sources contain images, sound, video, animation, and/or text; text-only sources contain only the text. 3. A dictionary that includes only the words most frequently used in a language. 4. A reference source that contains synonyms for commonly used words. 5. General, single-volume, encyclopedias for children and young adults, and subject encyclopedias. 6. CD ROM and Internet. 7. Titles of articles, sections of articles, volume(s), page(s), visual aids, and where to look for more information. 8. Hyperlinked image used in a computer database. 9. A single-volume reference book containing facts on a wide range of topics. 10. A collection of maps. 11. Reference books that provide information about the lives and accomplishments of famous people, living or dead.

Interpreting Graphic Aids

OBJECTIVES

1. Teach students about the graphic aids found in textbooks and other sources of information.
2. Teach students to interpret the information found in graphic aids.

TITLES OF REPRODUCIBLE ACTIVITIES

8-1 Pictographs
8-2 Pie Graphs
8-3 Bar Graphs
8-4 Line Graphs
8-5 Diagrams
8-6 Tables
8-7 Organizational Charts
8-8 Flow Charts
8-9 Time Lines
8-10 Map Legend
8-11 Map Compass
8-12 Map Scale
8-13 Political and Physical Maps
8-14 Road Maps
8-15 Combining Types of Maps
8-16 Weather Maps
8-17 Chapter Eight Mastery Assessment
Answer Key

USING THE REPRODUCIBLE ACTIVITIES

After you have distributed a reproducible activity, here are suggestions for its use. Feel free to add further information, illustrations, or examples. Wherever possible, relate the activity to actual subject area assignments.

8-1 Pictographs

Tell students that graphs are used to show information. Explain that graphs show the relationship between two or more things. Tell students you will be teaching them about four types of graphs. Use this activity to introduce students to pictographs. Then have students use the pictograph to answer the questions.

8-2 Pie Graphs

Tell students the term *pie graph* is used because this type of graph looks like a pie divided into slices. Explain that the parts must add up to 100%. Also explain why some pie graphs have a part labeled "Others." Then have students use the pie graph to answer the questions.

8-3 Bar Graphs

Tell students that bar graphs are used to show the relationships between sets of facts. Show students the different parts of a bar graph. Review the directions for reading a bar graph. Have students follow these directions as they use the bar graph to answer the questions. Finally, point out that sometimes the bars are presented horizontally.

8-4 Line Graphs

Explain that line graphs are used to show trends over a period of time. Show students the different parts of a line graph. Review the directions for reading a line graph. Have students follow these directions as they use the line graph to answer the questions.

8-5 Diagrams

Bring out that diagrams show the parts of an object or thing. Point out that diagrams often show how the parts go together or how an object or thing works. Then have students use the diagram to answer the questions.

8-6 Tables

Tell students that tables are used to present facts. Explain the importance of the columns and column headings. Review the directions for reading a table. Have students follow these directions as they use the table to answer the questions.

8-7 Organizational Charts

Tell students that organizational charts show how things are organized. Explain how boxes and lines are used to present information and show relationships. Then have students use the organizational chart to answer the questions.

8-8 Flow Charts

Bring out that flow charts are used to show a process by which something works or occurs. Point out that arrows show the direction or order in which the process happens. Then have students use the flow chart to answer the questions.

8-9 Time Lines

Tell students that a time line shows the relationship between events over time and shows when important things happen. Point out that most time lines are shown from left to right. Review the directions for reading a time line. Have students follow these directions as they use the time line to answer the questions.

8-10 Map Legend

Tell students that maps have a legend that explains the symbols appearing on the map. Explain that map legends may vary from map to map. Tell students that sometimes a map legend is called a map key. Then have students use the map legend at the bottom of the map to answer the questions about the map shown.

8-11 Map Compass

Tell students that a map compass is used to show directions on a map. Then have students use the map compass to answer the questions about the map shown.

8-12 Map Scale

Explain that a map scale is used to find the distance between two places on a map. Map scales are often shown in both miles and kilometers. Use the steps provided in the activity to demonstrate how to find the distance between two cities. Then have students use the map scale to answer questions about the map shown.

8-13 Political and Physical Maps

Bring out the unique features of these two types of maps. Have students use what they learned to answer the questions.

8-14 Road Maps

Tell students that a road map shows both major highways and secondary roads. Show students the symbols used to mark the number of the major highways and secondary roads. Also show how major highways appear in darker or bolder ink than secondary roads. Explain how road maps are used when traveling. Then have students use the road map to answer the questions.

8-15 Combining Types of Maps

Review political, physical, and road maps and the use of a legend, compass, and scale. Have students use the map of California to answer the questions.

8-16 Weather Maps

Show how weather maps are used to show present weather conditions and predict future weather conditions. Have students use the weather map to answer the questions.

8-17 Chapter Eight Mastery Assessment

Have students complete this assessment at any point you believe they have learned to use and interpret graphic aids. Review the results of the assessment with the students. Provide additional instruction as necessary.

Pictographs use pictures or symbols to present information. Each picture or symbol stands for an amount of something. A pictograph has a title that tells you what it shows. It also has a key that explains what each picture stands for. Examine this pictograph and answer the questions.

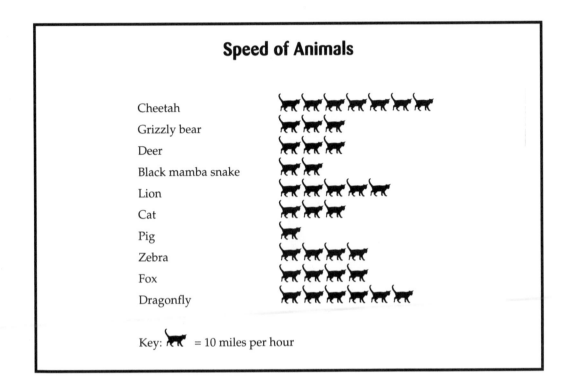

1. What does this pictograph show?

2. What does 🐈 stand for?

3. Which is the slowest animal?

4. Fastest animal?

5. Which animals can travel at 40 miles per hour?

6. Which animals travel faster than a deer?

7. Which animals travel slower than a grizzly bear?

8. What does 🐈🐈 stand for?

9. How many more miles per hour does a zebra travel than a dog?

10. Which animal travels twice as fast as a dog?

Pie graphs look like a pie divided into slices. The title tells the subject of the pie graph. Each part of a pie graph shows how much of the whole it stands for. The parts must equal the whole and must add up to 100 percent. Very small parts are often combined and called "Others." This is done because it is difficult to show a very small part of something.

Examine this pie graph and answer the questions.

Chemical Elements in the Human Body

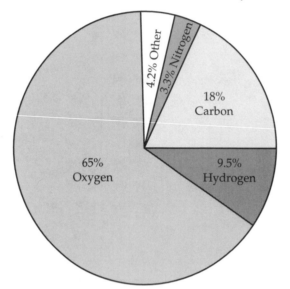

1. What does this pie graph show?

2. Which chemical is found in the greatest amount in the human body?

3. Is there a higher amount of hydrogen or carbon in the human body?

4. Oxygen plus carbon make up what percentage of the chemical elements in the human body?

5. About one-fifth of the chemical elements in the body consist of which element?

6. Oxygen and hydrogen combine to form water in the human body. About what percentage of the human body is water?

7. The parts shown in a pie graph must add up to what percentage?

8. Why is there a category called "Others"?

Bar graphs use bars to show the relationships between sets of facts. A bar graph has a title at the top and labels on the left-hand side and bottom. On the bottom of the graph there is a number line. The length of each bar shows how much the bar stands for.

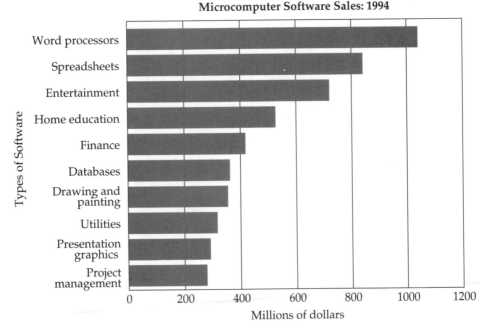

Source: U.S. government

Look at the bar graph and read the directions for interpreting bar graphs. Use what you learn to answer the questions.

Directions for reading a bar graph:

- Read the title to learn what it is about.
- Read the label on the left-hand side to learn what each bar stands for.
- Read the label at the bottom to learn what the numbers stand for.
- Look at the length of any one bar to learn about a specific thing.
- Look at the length of two or more bars to make comparisons between things.

1. What is this bar graph about?

2. What do the bars stand for?

3. What do the numbers stand for?

4. Which type of software sold the most in 1994?

5. For which type of software were sales about $400 million?

6. Which sold more, entertainment or database software?

7. What were the combined sales for home education and finance software?

Line Graphs

Line graphs are used to show trends over a period of time. A line graph has a title at the top and labels on the left-hand side and at the bottom. On the left side of the line graph there is a number line. Dots are used to show how much there is of something. The dots are connected by a line. The line shows how a trend is developing or how things are changing. Look at the following line graph:

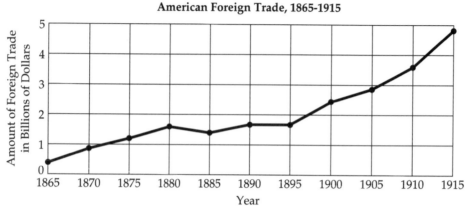

American Foreign Trade, 1865-1915

Source: U.S. government

Look at the line graph and read the directions for interpreting line graphs. Use what you learned to answer the questions.

Directions for reading a line graph:

- Read the title to learn what it is about.
- Read the label at the bottom to learn what the dots stand for.
- Read the label on the left-hand side to learn what the numbers stands for.
- Look at any one dot to learn about a specific thing.
- Look at the line to see the trend of how things are changing.

1. What is the line graph about?

2. What do the dots stand for?

3. What do the numbers on the left-hand side stand for?

4. What was the amount of foreign trade in 1880?

5. 1905?

6. 1915?

7. What happened to the amount of foreign trade from 1875 to 1880?

8. 1880–1885?

9. During which five-year period was foreign trade greatest?

10. What was the trend in foreign trade from 1865 to 1915?

Diagrams are drawings of an object or thing. A diagram shows the parts of the object or thing. The parts are labeled. Often a diagram shows how the parts go together or how the object or thing works. Look at the following diagram and answer the questions.

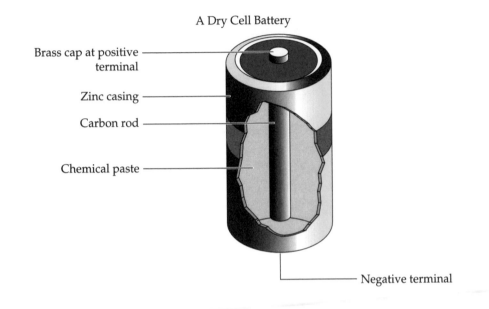

A Dry Cell Battery

Brass cap at positive terminal

Zinc casing

Carbon rod

Chemical paste

Negative terminal

1. What is the title of this diagram?

2. How many parts of the battery are shown?

3. Which part is in the center of the battery?

4. Which part is at the top of the battery?

5. Which part is at the bottom of the battery?

6. Which part is on the outside of the battery?

7. What is the material called that surrounds the carbon rod?

Tables are used to present facts. A table has a title that explains its purpose. In the table you will find columns. Each column has a heading that tells what facts you will find in that column. Look at the following table and answer the questions.

The Sun and Its Planets

Names of Planets	Miles from Sun	Orbit Time
Mercury	36 million	88 days
Venus	67 million	224 days
Earth	93 million	365.25 days
Mars	142 million	687 days
Jupiter	483 million	11.9 years
Saturn	887 million	29.5 years
Uranus	1,783 million	84 years
Neptune	2,794 million	164.8 years
Pluto	3,666 million	247.7 years

1. What is the title of this table?

2. What information is presented in the first column?

3. Second column?

4. Third column?

5. How many miles is Earth from the sun?

6. How many miles is Neptune from the sun?

7. How long does it take Earth to orbit around the sun?

8. Which planet has the shortest orbit?

9. Which the longest?

10. Which planet is farthest from the sun?

11. Which two planets are closer to the sun than Earth?

Organizational charts are used to show how things are organized. Information is presented in boxes. Each box is labeled to show what it presents. Lines are used to show how the boxes are related.

Look at the following organizational chart. It shows how the U.S. government is organized to do its work. The boxes contain facts about the government. The lines show how the facts go together. By studying the chart you can see how the government works.

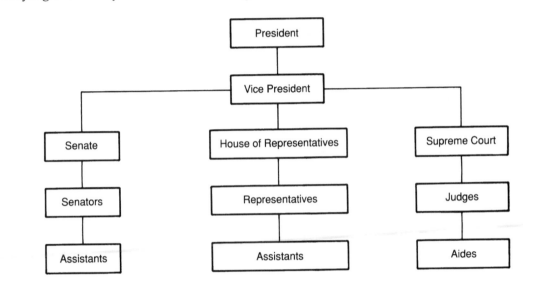

Use the chart to answer these questions:

1. Who is the highest ranking official in the United States government?

2. Who works in the Senate?

3. Who works in the House of Representatives?

4. Who works in the Supreme Court?

5. What official is directly below the president?

6. Where do aides work?

7. For whom do assistants work?

Flow charts are used to show a process by which something works or happens. Information is presented with drawings and arrows. Statements are used to show what is happening at each stage in the process. The arrows show the direction or order in which the process happens.

Look at the flow chart. It shows how paper is made from wood. Read the title and the statements. Study the drawings. Use the arrows to learn the order of the steps in the process of turning wood into paper. Then answer the questions.

How Wood Becomes Paper

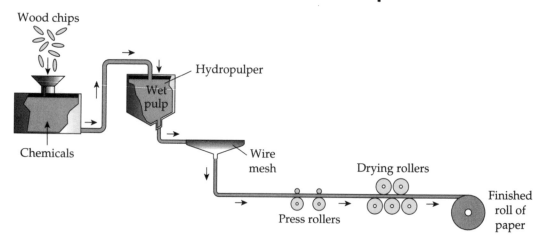

1. What is the title?

2. What process is being shown in this flow chart?

3. What is the first step in the process?

4. Second step?

5. Third step?

6. Fourth step?

7. What product is produced at the end of this process?

Time Lines

A time line shows the relationship between events over time. It also shows when important events happened. Most time lines run from left to right. The left-hand side of the time line is the earliest time and the right-hand side is the latest time.

Major Events of the U.S. Civil War

1861———————— 1862 ——————— 1863 ——————— 1864 ——————— 1865
Civil War begins   Ironclad ships   Battle of   Grant named   Confederates
as Confederates   Monitor and   Gettysburg   Commander   surrender
fire on Fort Sumter   Merrimac battle   Union Army

Look at the time line and read the directions for interpreting time lines. Use what you learn to answer the questions.

Directions for interpreting a time line:

- Read the title to learn what it is about.
- Identify the time period shown in the time line.
- Identify into what time periods the time line is divided.
- Study the information in the time line to learn how events are related over time.

1. What is the title?

2. What time period is shown?

3. In what time periods is the time line divided?

4. What was the first major event?

5. The last?

6. In what year did the battle of Gettysburg occur?

7. What event occurred the year before the battle of Gettysburg?

8. In what year did the Civil War begin? End?

A **map legend** tells you the meaning of each symbol used on a map. Because different maps contain different information, the symbols may be different from map to map. This means that the legend is different from map to map. On some maps, the map legend is called a **map key**. A map legend is usually at the bottom of a map.

Use this map and its legend to answer the questions that follow.

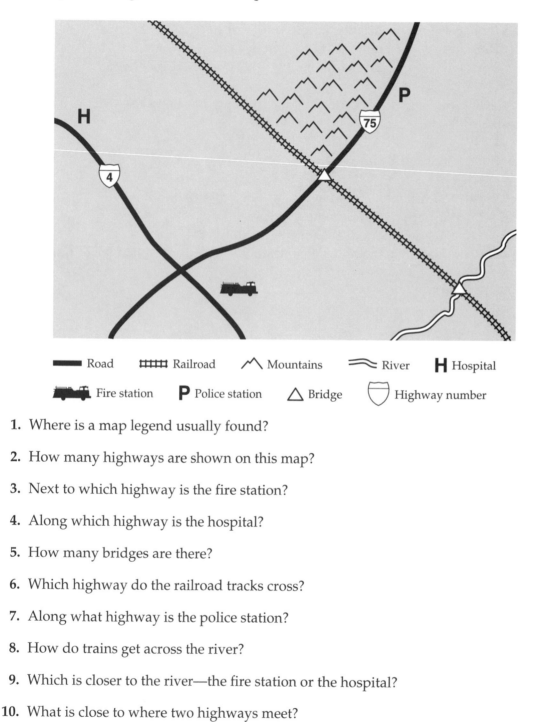

1. Where is a map legend usually found?

2. How many highways are shown on this map?

3. Next to which highway is the fire station?

4. Along which highway is the hospital?

5. How many bridges are there?

6. Which highway do the railroad tracks cross?

7. Along what highway is the police station?

8. How do trains get across the river?

9. Which is closer to the river—the fire station or the hospital?

10. What is close to where two highways meet?

A map compass shows you directions on a map. It shows you north (N), south (S), east (E), west (W), and the directions in between: northeast (NE), southeast (SE), and so on. Use the map of Arkansas and the map compass to answer the questions that follow.

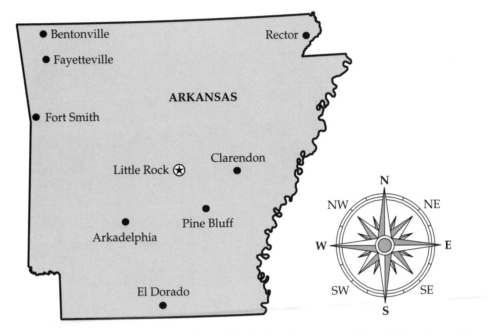

In what direction would you travel to go from Little Rock to each of the following cities.

1. Fayetteville?

2. El Dorado?

3. Clarendon?

4. Rector?

In what direction would you travel if you went from

5. Pine Bluff to Arkadelphia?

6. Bentonville to Ft. Smith?

7. El Dorado to Little Rock?

8. Fort Smith to Rector?

Which city is furthest

9. east?

10. west?

11. north?

12. south?

Map Scale

The map scale shows distance on a map. It may tell distance in miles, in kilometers, or in both miles and kilometers. You should use the map scale to find how far it is from one place to another.

Here is a map containing cities and a map scale:

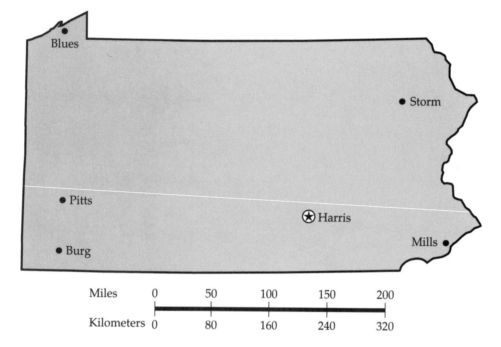

Here are the steps to follow to find the distance between two cities:

- Place the edge of a piece of paper between any two cities shown on the map.
- Make a mark on the paper by each city.
- Lay the paper on the scale to find how far it is between the two marks. This will tell you how far it is between the two cities.

Follow these steps to answer these questions.

1. How many kilometers are equal to 100 miles?

2. How many miles is it from Mills to Pitts? How many kilometers?

3. How many miles is it from Blues to Pitts? How many kilometers?

4. How far is it between Blues and Harris in miles?

5. How far is it between Harris and Storm in kilometers?

6. Which two cities are closest? How many miles is it from one to the other?

7. Which two cities are farthest apart? How many kilometers is it from one to the other?

8. Which two cities are farther apart—Burg and Pitts, or Storm and Pitts?

A **political map** has lines that show political or government boundaries. Look at the political map of South America, which shows the countries on this continent.

A **physical map** shows the features of the earth's surface such as mountains, highlands, plateaus, deserts, and major bodies of water. Look at the physical map of South America and find these features. No political boundaries are shown.

Political Map of South America   Physical Map of South America

Which type of map would you use to:

1. identify the provinces in Canada?

2. identify major mountain ranges?

3. write a report on the major oceans in the world?

4. answer a question about the new countries in eastern Europe?

5. locate the Nile River?

6. learn which countries border France?

Road Maps

A **road map** shows the major highways and the secondary roads for a geographical area. The major highways are identified with dark lines and the secondary roads with light lines. Both types of roads have symbols showing the number or name of the highway or road. Road maps are used to show how to get from one place to another. Here is a sample road map.

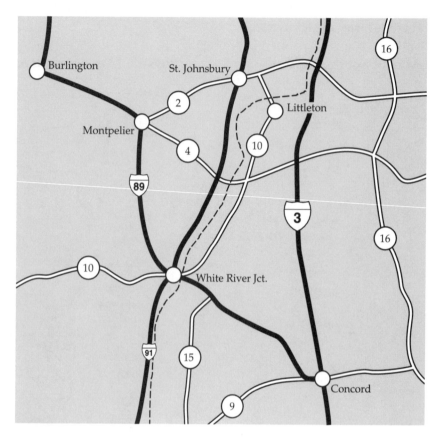

1. What do dark lines identify?

2. Light lines?

3. What major highway would you take to travel between Burlington and Concord?

4. What direct route takes you from Concord to Littleton?

5. What community do you find where 91 and 2 meet?

6. What community do you find where routes 10, 89, and 91 cross.

7. What two major highways will take you to Concord?

8. How many highways are shown? What are their numbers?

9. How many secondary roads? What are their numbers?

10. Does a highway pass through Littleton?

Here is a map of California that combines the features from political, physical, and road maps. It has a legend, compass, and scale. Use the map to answer the questions.

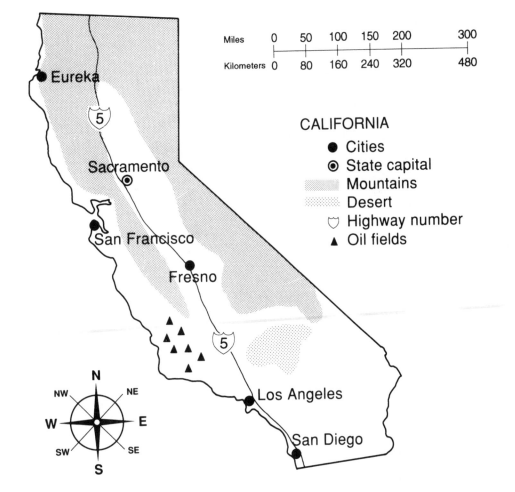

1. Between which two cities are oil fields located?

2. What is the distance in kilometers between San Francisco and Los Angeles?

3. What is the state capital?

4. In which direction would you travel from San Francisco to Fresno?

5. What highway runs north and south?

Maps can be used to tell information about the weather. Use the legend and compass to answer the questions.

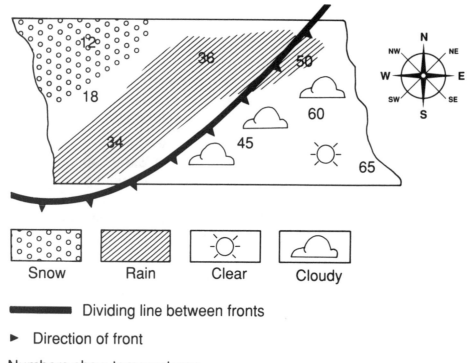

Snow   Rain   Clear   Cloudy

━━━━━━ Dividing line between fronts

► Direction of front

Numbers show temperatures

What is the predicted weather for these areas?

1. SE

2. NE

3. NW

4. SW

5. In which area is the coldest temperature?

6. In which area is the warmest temperature?

7. What will the weather be like in the SE area in a day or two?

Directions: Show what you have learned about using and interpreting graphic aids by writing an answer for each of the following:

1. What is used to show an amount of something in a pictograph?

2. In a pie graph, what must the parts equal?

3. What do bar graphs show?

4. What type of graph is used to show trends over a period of time?

5. What type of drawing shows the parts of some object or thing?

6. What type of graphic aid shows facts arranged in columns?

7. What type of chart shows how things are organized?

8. What type of chart shows how something works?

9. What type of graphic aid is used to show when important events happened?

10. Tell what each type of map shows:

    a. Political

    b. Physical

    c. Road

    d. Weather

11. What is each of the following used for on a map?

    a. Legend

    b. Compass

    c. Scale

8-1 1. Speed of animals. 2. 10 mph. 3. Pig. 4. Cheetah. 5. Zebra and fox. 6. Cheetah, lion, zebra, fox, and dragonfly. 7. Black mamba snake and pig. 8. 20 mph. 9. 10 mph. 10. Dragonfly.

8-2 1. Chemical elements in the human body. 2. Oxygen. 3. Carbon. 4. 83%. 5. Carbon. 6. 75%. 7. 100%. 8. Because it is difficult to show very small parts.

8-3 1. Microcomputer software sales in 1994. 2. Types of software. 3. Sales in millions of dollars. 4. Word processors. 5. Finance. 6. Entertainment. 7. About 900 million dollars.

8-4 1. American foreign trade from 1865–1915. 2. How much foreign trade there was. 3. Amount of foreign trade in billions of dollars. 4. About 1.5 billion dollars. 5. About 2.9 billion dollars. 6. About 4.9 billion dollars. 7. Increased. 8. Decreased slightly. 9. 1910–1915. 10. Increased.

8-5 1. A Dry Cell Battery. 2. 5. 3. Carbon rod. 4. Brass cap. 5. Negative terminal. 6. Zinc casing. 7. Chemical paste.

8-6 1. The Sun and Its Planets. 2. Names of planets. 3. Miles from sun. 4. Orbit time. 5. 93 million. 6. 2,794 million. 7. 365.25 days. 8. Mercury. 9. Pluto. 10. Pluto. 11. Mercury and Venus.

8-7 1. President. 2. Senators and assistants. 3. Representatives and assistants. 4. Judges and aides. 5. Vice-president. 6. Supreme Court. 7. Senators and representatives.

8-8 1. How Wood Becomes Paper. 2. The process by which wood is turned into paper. 3. Putting wood chips into the chemical container. 4. Making wet pulp in the Hydropulper. 5. Running the wet pulp through the wire mesh. 6. Running the wet pulp through the press rollers. 7. Roll of paper.

8-9 1. Major Events of the U.S. Civil War. 2. 1861–1865. 3. One year. 4. Confederates fire on Fort Sumter and war begins. 5. Confederates surrender. 6. 1863. 7. Battle between Monitor and Merrimac. 8. 1861, 1865.

8-10 1. Bottom of a map. 2. Two. 3. Highway 4. 4. Highway 4. 5. Two. 6. Highway 75. 7. Highway 75. 8. Cross a bridge. 9. Fire station. 10. Fire station.

8-11 1. NW. 2. S. 3. E. 4. NE. 5. W. 6. S. 7. N. 8. NE. 9. Rector. 10. Fort Smith. 11. Bentonville. 12. El Dorado.

8-12 1. 160 kilometers. 2. Approximately 340 miles, 530 kilometers. 3. Approximately 145 miles, 230 kilometers. 4. Approximately 260 miles. 5. Approximately 220 kilometers. 6. Pitts and Burg; approximately 45 miles. 7. Blues and Mills. Approximately 590 kilometers. 8. Storm and Pitts.

8-13 1. Political map. 2. Physical map. 3. Physical map. 4. Political map. 5. Physical map. 6. Political map.

8-14 1. Major highways. 2. Secondary roads. 3. Highway 89. 4. Highway 3. 5. St. Johnsbury. 6. White River Junction. 7. Highways 3 and 89. 8. Three highways: 89, 91, 3. 9. Six secondary roads: 2, 16, 4, 10, 15, 9. 10. No, a road does.

8-15 1. San Francisco and Los Angeles. 2. Approximately 580 kilometers. 3. Sacramento. 4. SE. 5. Highway 5.

8-16 1. Clear. 2. Cloudy and rain. 3. Snow. 4. Rain. 5. NW. 6. SE. 7. Cloudy, possible rain turning to snow, colder.

8-17 1. Pictures or symbols.   2. The whole (100%).   3. Relationships between sets of facts.   4. Line graph.   5. Diagram.   6. Table.   7. Organizational chart.   8. Flow chart.   9. Time line.   10. a. Political or government boundaries.   b. Features of the earth's surface.   c. Major highways and secondary roads.   d. Current and predicted weather.   11. a. To explain the symbols on a map.   b. Tells directions on a map.   c. Tells distance on a map.

CHAPTER NINE

Writing a Research Paper

OBJECTIVES

1. Teach students a strategy for writing a research paper.
2. Teach students how to identify, locate, and document information needed to write a research paper.

TITLES OF REPRODUCIBLE ACTIVITIES

USING THE REPRODUCIBLE ACTIVITIES

After you have distributed a reproducible activity, here are suggestions for its use. Define any terms and clarify any concepts students do not know.

Feel free to add further information, illustrations, or examples. Wherever possible, relate the activity to actual subject-area assignments.

9-1 A Strategy for Writing a Research Paper

Use the activities in this chapter to take students through the steps of writing a research paper. Students should develop their papers as they move through the activities.

Have students take notes as you elaborate on each of the ten steps in writing a research paper presented in 9-1.

9-2 Learning about Choosing a Topic

Use the introductory text to help students learn about topics that are too broad, too narrow, or just right. Have students explain why each topic is too broad, too narrow, or just right.

The first topic is too broad because there is an unlimited amount of information available about space flight. It would take students a very long time to locate all the sources, read them, and then write a paper within the number of pages assigned.

The second topic is too narrow because it focuses on one very specific aspect of space flight. Students will find it difficult to find enough information to write a paper.

The third topic is just right because there is enough information available to write a paper, but not so much that the students will be overwhelmed by the amount of information.

9-3 Practice Choosing a Topic

Review with students what they have learned in 9-2. Then have students use this activity to identify topics as too broad, too narrow, or just right.

9-4 Knowing If You Have Chosen a Good Topic

Have students answer the four questions for the topics they wrote. Then have students choose one of their topic statements as the best one for their research papers. Have students explain why they chose that topic statement.

9-5 Locating Sources of Information

Use this activity to familiarize students with the process of finding information in various sources. Students learned about these sources of information in Chapters Five, Six, and Seven. If necessary, quickly review these sources. Students will have to go to the library to complete this activity. Encourage them to look for electronic sources of information such as on CD ROM. Eliminate the web page as a source if students do not have access to the WWW in your school.

9-6 Preparing Bibliography Cards
9-7 Preparing Bibliography Cards for Electronic Sources

Explain the importance of using bibliography cards to document sources of information used when writing research papers. Tell students they must prepare a separate bibliography card for each source of information, whether print or electronic. Use the sample cards to explain how bibliography cards are prepared for each type of source of information. Point out that for a given information source, the citation may not include all the parts called for on a bibliography card. For example, the author might not be identified.

Point out that information for bibliography cards for electronic sources comes from the computer record. The headings on a computer record will not necessarily match the headings required for a bibliography card. Students will have to match the information on a computer record with the information needed for a bibliography card.

Have students prepare bibliography cards for the six types of sources of information found in 9-5.

9-8 Preparing Note Cards

Explain to students why they need to prepare note cards. Have students refer to the sample bibliography card and the note cards that go with it. Tell students that they must follow the five steps as they prepare note cards for their papers.

As students follow these five steps, point out that articles such as *the*, *a*, and *an* should not be considered the first word when alphabetizing. Emphasize the need for legible writing. Remind students to use abbreviations, acronyms, and other brief forms to reduce the amount of text they write.

Have students use what they learned to prepare note cards for their papers.

9-9 Writing the Outline

Explain to students why they need to prepare an outline. Have students refer to the sample outline. Tell students that they must follow the seven steps as they prepare an outline for their papers.

Have students use what they learned to prepare outlines for their papers.

9-10 Writing the Draft

Tell students to write a draft of their research papers. Use the text and sample pages to explain the parts of a research paper that must be included in a draft. Point out that not all sections of a research paper are included in a draft. The title page (9-12), table of contents (9-13), and bibliography (9-14) will be added when preparing the final paper.

Have students follow the five steps to write the drafts of their research papers. Tell them they must double space their drafts to leave room for revisions.

9-11 Revising the Draft

Show students how to use the Revising Checklist to revise their drafts.

9-12 Preparing the Title Page

Use the introductory text and sample title page to explain what a title page contains and how to prepare it. Then have students prepare title pages for their papers.

9-13 Preparing the Table of Contents

Use the introductory text and sample table of contents to explain what a table of contents contains and how to prepare it. Have students prepare tables of contents for their papers.

9-14 Preparing the Bibliography

Use the introductory text and sample bibliography to explain what a bibliography is and how to prepare it. Have students prepare bibliographies for their papers.

9-15 Final Checklist

Discuss with students how to use the Final Checklist to be sure their papers are ready to hand in. Then have students complete the Final Checklist. Help students to make any revisions necessary until they can answer yes to all the questions.

9-16 Chapter Nine Mastery Assessment

Have students complete this assessment at any point you feel they have learned the ten steps in writing a research paper. Review the results of the assessment with the students. Provide additional instruction as necessary.

Here are the most important steps to follow to write a research paper. As your teacher tells you about each step, write down the important things you need to remember.

Step 1:   Choose a topic.

Step 2:   Locate sources of information.

Step 3:   Prepare bibliography cards.

Step 4:   Prepare note cards.

Step 5:   Write the outline.

Step 6:   Write the paper.

Step 7:   Prepare a bibliography.

Step 8:   Prepare a title page.

Step 9:   Prepare a table of contents.

Step 10:   Check your paper before handing it in to your teacher.

The first step in writing a research paper is to choose a topic. If the topic you choose is **too broad**, there will be too much information to find, read, and understand in the time you have available to complete the paper. If the topic you choose is **too narrow**, you will not find enough information to write about. You must choose a topic that is **just right**. This means that you can find enough sources to complete your paper in the time you have available. It also means that you can write your paper within the number of pages assigned by your teacher.

1. The following topic is too broad. Write a statement telling why.

   Topic: **The history of space flight.**

2. The following topic is too narrow. Write a statement telling why.

   Topic: **Reentry to the earth's atmosphere during space flight.**

3. The following topic is just right. Write a statement telling why.

   Topic: **Space flight to the moon.**

Read the first set of topics. One topic is too broad, one is too narrow, and one is just right. Write *too broad*, *too narrow*, or *just right* below each topic. Do the same for the sets that follow.

1. The role of nurses at the Battle of Gettysburg

   The Civil War

   Battle of Gettysburg

2. Mammals in the sea

   Orcas in Alaska

   Migrating whales

3. Buddhism

   Religions of the world

   Buddhist monks in training

Here are some important questions you should answer about any topic you choose. These questions will help you know if the topic you have chosen is a good one.

Write at least two topics about which you would like to write a research paper.

Topic 1

Topic 2

Topic 3

For each topic, answer questions 1–4 on a separate piece of paper.

1. *Is the topic too broad, too narrow, or just right?*

   Remember, if the topic is too broad or too narrow, you will find it difficult to complete the paper as required by your teacher.

2. *Does your library have enough information available on the topic?*

   Check in the library to see if there are enough sources on the topic. Make sure you have at least as many sources as required by your teacher.

3. *Are you interested in the topic?*

   Be sure to select a topic about which you are interested. It takes a lot of time to do the research and writing. If you are not interested in the topic, you will probably not do a very good job of writing the paper.

4. *Will your teacher approve the topic?*

   Show your written topic to your teacher and ask for approval. Do not begin to work on a topic unless your teacher has approved it.

5. Choose one of the topics approved by your teacher for your research paper. Write it here.

6. Why did you choose this topic?

In the space below, write the topic you selected in 9-4.

Find information on your topic in each of the following sources. For each source, write its title and call number. For the first five sources, also ✔ whether it is in Print or Electronic format. Include at least one source that is in electronic format.

1. **Encyclopedia Title:**

   Call Number: Print _____   Electronic _____

2. **Other Reference Book Title:**

   Call Number: Print _____   Electronic _____

3. **Book Title:**

   Call Number: Print _____   Electronic _____

4. **Magazine Title:**

   Call Number: Print _____   Electronic _____

5. **Newspaper Title:**

   Call Number: Print _____   Electronic _____

6. **Audiovisual Title:**

   Call Number:

7. **WWW Title of web page:**

   URL (address):

Bibliography cards are used to keep a record of the sources from which you obtained information for your paper. Look at how information is written on each bibliography card. Use these sample bibliography cards as models to prepare bibliography cards for sources you located in 9-5. You will learn about preparing bibliography cards for electronic sources in 9-7.

Encyclopedia

"Space Exploration." <u>Encyclopedia Americana</u>. 1995 ed.

Other Reference Book

Curtis, Anthony R. <u>Space Almanac: Facts, Figures, Names, Dates, Places, Lists, Charts, Tables, Maps Covering Space from Earth to the Edge of the Universe.</u> Woodsboro, MD: Arcsoft, 1989.

Book

Von Bencke, Matthew J. <u>The Politics of Space: A History of U.S.-Soviet/Russian Competition & Cooperation.</u> Boulder, CO: Westview Press, 1997.

Magazine Article

Steacy, Anne. "A Step in Time." <u>Macleans</u> 24 Jul. 1989: 47.

Newspaper Article

"Moon Landing Was Worth the Cost: (Results of CBS News Public Opinion Polls on Moon Landing in 1969)" <u>New York Times</u> 24 Jul. 1994, nat'l ed.: E5.

Audiovisual

<u>Moon Shot Videorecording: The Inside Story of the Apollo Project.</u> Prod. and Dir. Kirt Woltinger. Videocassette. TBS Productions Inc. Varied Directions International, Dist. Atlanta: Turner Home Entertainment, 1994.

Here is a sample bibliography card for a magazine article on CD ROM. You may also find articles from newspapers and encyclopedias on CD ROM. They may be full text or citation only. Headings are provided for each part of the citation shown on the sample card.

Electronic Database

Author(s):	Keefe, Ann.
Title of Article:	"July 20, 1969: The Greatest Adventure."
Title of Publication:	<u>Cobblestone: The History Magazine for Young People</u>
Date of Article/Page(s):	Jan. 1995: 36–41.
Title of Database:	<u>ProQuest Periodical Abstracts-Library</u>.
Publication Medium:	CD-ROM.
Name of Vendor:	UMI Company.
Date of CD ROM:	1996.

Here is a sample bibliography card for a web page found on the WWW. Headings are provided for each part of the citation shown on the sample card.

WWW Source

Author(s):	Dunbar, Brian.
Title:	<u>Apollo 11.</u>
Date of Information:	29 Mar. 1996.
Site:	National Aeronautics and Space Administration.
Address (URL):	http://www.nasa.gov/hqpao/apollo_11.html
Online Service:	World Wide Web, Netscape.
Date Accessed:	15 Mar. 1997.

Use these sample bibliography cards as models for preparing your own bibliography cards. Prepare bibliography cards for any of these types of sources you located in 9-5.

Look at the sample bibliography card and the note cards that go with it. Note cards are used to write notes or quotes from the source listed on the bibliography card. You must prepare one or more note cards for each bibliography card.

Sample Bibliography Card

Magazine Article ⑦

Steacy, Anne. "A Step in Time." <u>Macleans</u> 24 Jul. 1989: 47.

Sample Note Cards

⑦-1
President Nixon said "Because of what you have done, the heavens have become part of man's world." p47
Pope Paul VI cautioned not to put human achievement above God's.

⑦-2
It took $26 billion dollars and 8 yrs after JFK set goal.
1969–72—9 astro reached the moon
VP Agnew predicted man on Mars

Follow these steps as you prepare note cards for your paper.

Step 1:   Arrange your bibliography cards in alphabetical order by the first word on the card.

Step 2:   Number your bibliography cards starting with 1 for the first card. Write the number in the upper right-hand corner as in the sample bibliography card.

Step 3:   Number your note cards using two numbers separated by a dash as in the sample note cards. Write the number in the upper right-hand corner. In the sample note card numbered 7-1, 7 shows that the notes are for the source listed on bibliography card 7, and -1 shows this is the first card used to record notes from this source. A second note card would be numbered 7-2, and so on.

Step 4:   Circle the numbers on the note cards to keep them separate from other numbers you might write when taking notes.

Step 5:   Write notes on the note cards. Use your own words whenever possible. Place quotation marks around all quotes. Write the page number on which each quote appears.

Look at the sample outline for a research paper. It shows how to organize information from your note cards into main topics, subtopics, details, and subdetails.

Space Flight to the Moon

I. Manned space programs
   A. U.S. programs
      1. Mercury, Gemini, Apollo
         a. Apollo 11
   B. Soviet programs
      1. Vostok, Voskhod, Soyuz
   C. Accidents and other setbacks
      1. 1967 accidents
         a. Apollo
         b. Soyuz
      2. Apollo 13
II. The U.S.–Soviet race for the moon
   A. The cost of competition
      1. How much did it all cost?
      2. Was it worth it?
   B. Comparing technology
III. Looking back to the first step
   A. Anniversary celebrations
   B. Lunar projects since Apollo 17

Follow these steps as you prepare an outline for your paper.

Step 1:   Write the title of the research paper.

Step 2:   Organize the notes from your note cards into main topics.

Step 3:   Write the Roman numeral I and after it the first main topic. Write the Roman numeral II for the second main topic, and so on.

Step 4:   Write the subtopics that go with the first main topic. Use capital letters before each subtopic.

Step 5:   Write the details that go with each of these subtopics. Use Arabic numerals before each detail.

Step 6:   Write the subdetails that go with each of these details. Use small letters before each subdetail.

Step 7:   Repeat Steps 4, 5, and 6 for each main topic.

A **draft** is a paper you write that must be revised before it becomes your final paper. Read about the parts of a research paper that you must include in your draft. Look at the sample pages that show where the parts are located in the research paper. Follow these steps as you write a draft of your research paper.

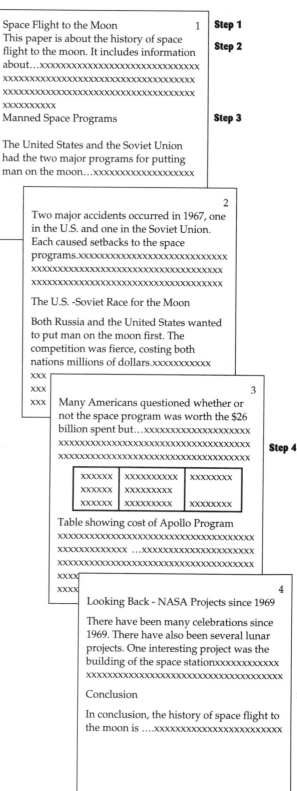

Step 1: Write the title at the top of the page. The title is a short statement that tells the subject of your paper.

Step 2: Write an introduction that introduces the topic and tells the reader what your paper will be about. The introduction is a paragraph or two at the beginning of a paper.

Step 3: Write the body of your paper. It begins after the introduction and ends before the conclusion. The body includes headings and the text that goes with them. The body is the longest part of the paper, usually several pages.

Step 4: Insert any pictures, drawings, charts, and other visual aids that will help the reader understand what you are writing about in your paper.

Step 5: Write a conclusion. The conclusion tells the reader what you have learned about the topic or summarizes your point of view.

Use the **Revising Checklist** to learn what changes you may need to make in the draft of your paper. Place a ✔ next to each question for which you can answer YES. Revise your draft until you can check Yes to all the questions.

Revising Checklist

_____ 1. Does the introduction clearly introduce the topic?

_____ 2. Did I include headings to help the reader understand the topic?

_____ 3. Does the body of the paper contain all facts needed?

_____ 4. Does each paragraph contain a main idea?

_____ 5. Does every paragraph and sentence add something to the paper?

_____ 6. Did I choose the best words to explain ideas?

_____ 7. Does my conclusion follow from the facts?

_____ 8. Did I spell all words correctly?

_____ 9. Did I capitalize words as needed?

_____ 10. Is there subject-verb agreement in all cases?

_____ 11. Are tenses consistent?

_____ 12. Are all sentences complete?

_____ 13. Did I use quotation marks to identify all quotations?

_____ 14. Did I number the pages correctly?

_____ 15. Do I have a one-inch margin at the top, bottom, and both sides?

_____ 16. Have I reread the paper several times to find ways to improve it?

The **title page** is the first page of the research paper. It must include the title of the paper, the name of the writer, the name of the teacher, and the date the paper is due.

Look at the sample title page. Follow these steps to prepare a title page for your paper.

1. Center and type the title. Use all caps or bold to highlight it.

2. Three lines below the title, center and type the word *by*. Three lines below the word *by*, center and type your name.

3. Two lines below your name, center and type the date that the paper is due.

4. Four lines from the bottom margin, center and type *For*: followed by your teacher's name.

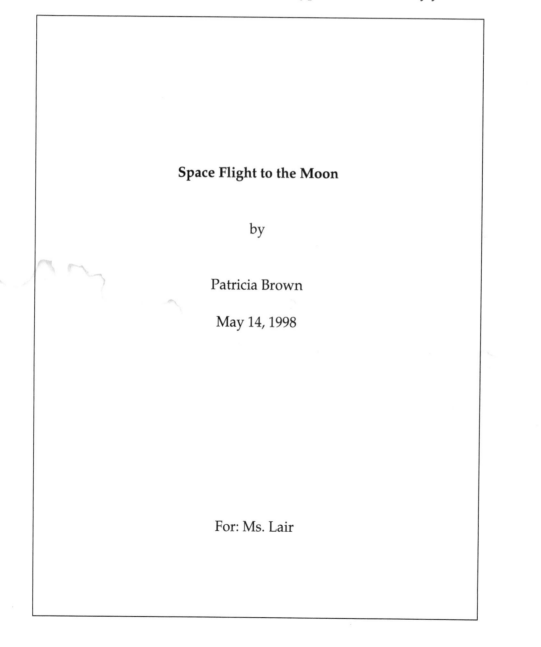

Space Flight to the Moon

by

Patricia Brown

May 14, 1998

For: Ms. Lair

The **table of contents** is the second page of the research paper. It must include the introduction, all headings, conclusion, and bibliography.

Look at the sample table of contents. Follow these steps to prepare a table of contents for your paper.

1. Type "Table of Contents" at the top of a page with the first letter of the word "Table" and the first letter of the word "Contents" capitalized.

2. Type each entry and the page number on which it begins. Capitalize the major words in each entry.

3. Use dashes or dots to connect the entry to its page number.

Table of Contents

	Page
Introduction	1
Manned Space Programs	1
U.S. Programs	2
Soviet Programs	3
Accidents	4
The U.S.–Soviet Race for the Moon	5
The Cost of Space Flight to the Moon	6
Technology	6
NASA Projects Since 1969	7
Conclusion	7
Bibliography	8

The **bibliography** provides a list of all the sources you used to gather information for the paper. It is included at the end of your paper.

Look at the sample bibliography. Follow these steps to prepare a bibliography for your paper.

1. Type the word **Bibliography** at the top of a page in the center.

2. Put your bibliography cards in alphabetical order by the first word on each card.

3. Type the information as it appears on each bibliography card. Indent the second and following lines as shown on the sample bibliography.

Bibliography

Curtis, Anthony R. <u>Space Almanac: Facts, Figures, Names, Dates, Places, Lists, Charts, Tables, Maps Covering Space from Earth to the Edge of the Universe</u>. Woodsboro, MD:Arcsoft, 1989.

Dunbar, Brian. <u>Apollo 11</u>. 29 Mar. 1996. National Aeronautics and Space Administration. http://www.nasa.gov/hqpao/apollo_11.html World Wide Web, Netscape. 15 Mar. 1997.

Keefe, Ann. "July 20, 1969: The Greatest Adventure." <u>Cobblestone: The History Magazine for Young People</u> Jan. 1995: 36–41. <u>ProQuest Periodical Abstracts-Library</u>. CD-ROM . UMI Company, 1996.

"Moon Landing Was Worth the Cost: (Results of CBS News Public Opinion Polls on Moon Landing in 1969)" <u>New York Times</u> 24 Jul. 1994, nat'l ed.: E5.

<u>Moon Shot Videorecording: The Inside Story of the Apollo Project</u>. Prod. and Dir. Kirt Woltinger. Videocassette. TBS Productions Inc. Varied Directions International, Dist. Atlanta: Turner Home Entertainment, 1994.

"Space Exploration." <u>Encyclopedia Americana</u>. 1995 ed.

Steacy, Anne. "A Step in Time." <u>Macleans</u> 24 Jul. 1989: 47.

Von Bencke, Matthew J. <u>The Politics of Space: A History of U.S.–Soviet/Russian Competition & Cooperation</u>. Boulder, CO: Westview Press, 1997.

When you have finished writing your research paper, look it over to complete the **Final Checklist**. Place a ✔ next to each question for which you can answer YES. If you have a ✔ next to all questions, your paper is ready to be handed in to your teacher. If not, revise your paper until you have a ✔ next to all questions. Then your paper is ready to be handed in.

Final Checklist

_____ 1. Do I have a title page?

_____ 2. Do I have a table of contents?

_____ 3. Are the pages numbered correctly?

_____ 4. Do I have a bibliography?

_____ 5. Do I have a second copy for myself?

_____ 6. Do I have a folder in which to place the original copy to hand in to my teacher?

See what you have learned about writing a research paper.

1. How many important steps must you follow to write a research paper?

2. What problem will you have if you choose a topic that is too broad? Too narrow?

3. List seven types of sources that you may use to locate information for your topic.

4. What is the purpose of bibliography cards?

5. On a note card, what does **6-2** mean?

6. Label each part of the following outline:

    I. _____

       A. _____

          1. _____

             a. _____

7. What is the first page of the research paper called? The second page?

8. What is a bibliography?

9. What is the purpose of the Final Checklist?

9-1 Notes will vary.

9-2 Responses will vary but should include these ideas: 1. Too much information to find, read, and understand.   2. Not enough information to write about.   3. The right number of sources to write a paper within time and length constraints.

9-3 1. Too narrow, too broad, just right.   2. Too broad, too narrow, just right.   3. Just right, too broad, too narrow.

9-4 Responses will vary.

9-5 Responses will vary.

9-6 Bibliography cards will vary.

9-7 Bibliography cards will vary.

9-8 Note cards will vary.

9-9 Outlines will vary.

9-10 Drafts will vary.

9-11 Responses will vary.

9-12 Title pages will vary.

9-13 Tables of contents will vary.

9-14 Bibliographies will vary.

9-15 Responses will vary.

9-16 1. Ten.   2. Will not be able to complete the paper in the number of pages assigned; will not be able to find enough information.   3. Encyclopedia; other reference book; book; magazine; newspaper; audiovisual; web page from the WWW.   4. To keep a record of the sources of information used for the paper.   5. Bibliography card 6, note card 2.

6. I. Main Topic
    A. Subtopic
       1. Detail
         a. Subdetail

7. Title Page; Table of Contents.   8. A list of all the sources used to gather information for a paper.   9. To be sure a paper is ready to be handed in.

CHAPTER 10

Preparing for and Taking Tests

OBJECTIVES

1. Teach students a five-day strategy for preparing to take tests.
2. Teach students the DETER strategy for taking tests.
3. Teach students how to do well on multiple-choice, true/false, matching, and completion tests.
4. Teach students the QUOTE strategy for taking essay tests.

TITLES OF REPRODUCIBLE ACTIVITIES

USING THE REPRODUCIBLE ACTIVITIES

10-1 Preparing for Tests

Tell students that to do well on a test, they must be prepared. Introduce students to the five-step plan they should follow to be prepared to take a test. Have students complete the activity.

10-2 Five-Day Test Preparation Plan

Introduce the five-day test preparation plan and review what must be done on each day. If necessary, review with students how notes are taken from textbooks (Chapter Two) and in class (Chapter Four), and how remembering strategies are used to remember information (Chapter One). Have students complete the activity.

10-3 Using the DETER Strategy to Do Well on a Test

Introduce the acronym DETER as a strategy for taking a test. Remind students that just remembering information for a test is not sufficient to do well on a test. They must also know how to take a test. Have students complete the activity.

10-4 Learning about Multiple-Choice Test Items

Use the sample items to explain two types of multiple-choice items. Then have students use the *information* provided to write a multiple-choice item for each type learned.

10-5 What to Do When Taking Multiple-Choice Tests

Use the statements to explain to students what they should do when taking multiple-choice tests. Have students write notes in the white space provided.

10-6 Practice Taking a Multiple-Choice Test

Review with students what they have learned about multiple-choice test items and taking multiple-choice tests. Then have students complete the test. Go over the answers with the students.

10-7 What to Do When Taking True/False Tests

Use the statements to explain to students what they should do when taking true/false tests. Have students write notes as needed.

10-8 Practice Taking a True/False Test

Review with students what they have learned about true/false tests. Then have students complete the test. Go over the answers with the students.

10-9 What to Do When Taking Matching Tests

Use the example of a matching test item to show one format in which matching test items appear. Explain other formats as appropriate for your students. For example, responses may be written next to words or terms in the first column, or there may be a different number of words and terms in each column.

Use the statements to explain to students what they should do when taking matching tests. Have students write notes as needed.

10-10 Practice Taking a Matching Test

Review with students what they have learned about taking matching tests. Then have students complete the two tests. Go over the answers with the students.

10-11 What to Do When Taking Completion Tests

Use the statements to explain to students what they should do when taking completion tests. Have students write notes as needed.

10-12 Practice Taking a Completion Test

Review with students what they have learned about taking completion tests. Then have students complete the test. Go over the answers with the students.

10-13 The QUOTE Strategy for Taking Essay Tests

Introduce QUOTE as a strategy for taking essay tests. Have students take notes as you explain each step in the strategy.

10-14 QUOTE: Question

Use the activity to explain the Question step in the QUOTE strategy for answering essay test items. Introduce the direction words *discuss, describe,* and *explain*. Have students place [   ] around direction words in the sample essay test items.

10-15 More Direction Words

Use this activity to familiarize students with additional direction words they will see in essay test items. Add additional information as needed. Have students select an appropriate direction word to complete each of the essay test items.

10-16 QUOTE: Underline

Use the activity to explain the Underline step in the QUOTE strategy for answering essay test items. For each item, have students bracket the direction word and underline the words that tell to what they must respond in the test item.

10-17 QUOTE: Organize/Write

Use the activity to explain the Organize/Write step in the QUOTE strategy for answering essay test items. Then review with students the procedures for writing one- and multiple-paragraph answers to essay test items. Finally, have students write a one paragraph answer to the essay test item that concludes the activity.

10-18 QUOTE: Time

Use the activity to explain the Time step in the QUOTE strategy for answering essay test items. Review with students the procedure for deciding how much time should be spent answering each test item. Finally, have students answer the questions to show what they have learned about planning their time when taking an essay test.

10-19 QUOTE: Evaluate

Use the activity to explain the Evaluate step in the QUOTE strategy for answering essay test items. Review with students the items for evaluating the content, writing, and mechanics of answers to essay test items. Then have students use the items to evaluate the answer they wrote to the essay test item in 10-17. Finally, based on their responses of *yes* or *no* to the items in 10-19, have students write a statement that tells how they could improve the answer they wrote for the essay test item in 10-17.

10-20 Chapter Ten Mastery Assessment

Have students complete this assessment at any point you believe they have learned how to prepare for and take the different types of tests presented in this chapter. Review the results of the assessment with students. Provide additional instruction as needed.

Here are five steps you should follow to be prepared to take a test. You will get higher scores on your tests if you follow these steps.

1. To do well on a test, you must begin to prepare early. Schedule your time so you have enough time to study for the test. Do not wait until the night before a test to begin studying. You will learn how to use a five-day test preparation plan in Activity 10-2.

2. Ask your teacher what the test will cover. Ask these two questions:

   - What will be covered on the test?
   - What will not be covered on the test?

3. Ask your teacher what type of test will be given.

4. Gather the information you need to study from your textbook notes, class notes, and teacher handouts. Ask your teacher to explain anything you do not understand.

5. Use the remembering strategies taught in Chapter One to help you remember the information you are studying.

Write a sentence that tells about each step you should follow to be prepared to take a test:

1.

2.

3.

4.

5.

You should begin studying for a test five days before the test. Follow this five-day plan to get a high score on your tests. Each day gets you more ready for the test. Here is what you should do on each of the five days:

Day 5   Read your textbook notes and class notes. Also look at any handouts your teacher has given you. Highlight the information in your notes and handouts that you must know and remember for the test.

Day 4   Use the remembering strategies taught in Chapter One to help you remember the information you identified on Day 5.

Day 3   Rewrite the information in a brief form using the fewest words you can. Use abbreviations and symbols wherever possible. Use the remembering strategies to review your rewritten notes at least twice on this day.

Day 2   Think of the questions your teacher might ask on the test. Write each question and its answer.

Day 1   This is the day you take your test. Review your rewritten notes from Day 3. Also review the questions and answers you prepared on Day 2. You can do this while eating breakfast or while riding to school. Just before the test, go over any information you are having difficulty remembering.

Think about what you should do each day of the five-day test preparation plan. For each day, write a sentence that tells what you will do on that day.

Day 5

Day 4

Day 3

Day 2

Day 1

Once you have learned the information, you are ready to take the test. However, you still need a strategy for taking the test. The **DETER** strategy can help you get high scores on your test. Here are the five test-taking steps the acronym **DETER** will help you remember.

D   Read the test **Directions** carefully. Ask your teacher to explain any part of the directions you do not understand.

E   **Examine** the entire test to see how much you have to do. Do this right after you have read and understood the test directions.

T   Decide how much **Time** you should spend answering each item on the test. See how many items are on the test and how many points each item is worth. Spend the most time answering the items that count the most points.

E   Begin by answering the items that are **Easiest** for you. Then answer as many of the remaining items as you can. Be sure to answer all the items if there is no penalty for wrong answers.

R   If you finish the test before time is up, **Review** your answers to make sure they are accurate and complete. Then you are ready to hand in your test.

Write a sentence that tells what each letter of the acronym **DETER** reminds you to do:

D

E

T

E

R

There are two types of multiple-choice test items.

The first type of multiple-choice item has a question followed by answer choices. You have to identify the answer choice that correctly answers the question. Look at the example:

Which holiday is observed to honor American soldiers killed during wars?

   a. Labor Day
   b. Presidents' Day
   c. Memorial Day
   d. Independence Day

The second type of multiple-choice item has an incomplete statement followed by answer choices. You have to identify the answer choice that correctly completes the statement. Look at the two examples:

On the last Monday in May, _____ is observed to honor American soldiers killed during wars.

   a. Labor Day
   b. Presidents' Day
   c. Memorial Day
   d. Independence Day

American soldiers killed during wars are honored on

   a. Labor Day
   b. Presidents' Day
   c. Memorial Day
   d. Independence Day

Use the following information to write a multiple-choice item for each type you just learned. Do this on your own paper.

   Information: There are 50 states in the United States.

What to Do When Taking Multiple-Choice Tests

Here are some things you should do to help you choose the correct answer choice for a multiple-choice item. Add information to each thing to do as your teacher discusses it with you.

- Read the question or statement and underline key words such as *not, all, some, except*. These words can give you clues to the correct answer.

- Read the question or statement along with each answer choice to help you decide which choice is correct.

- Once you decide an answer choice is incorrect, cross out the answer choice by drawing a line through it.

- If you crossed out all the answer choices except one, select the choice you did not cross out as your answer to the item.

- If you are left with more than one answer choice that you did not cross out, reread the question or statement with the remaining answer choices and choose the best answer.

- Answer all items unless there is a penalty for incorrect answers.

- Check your answers to make certain they are correct.

- Change an answer only if you are sure it is incorrect.

Take this multiple-choice test to show what you have learned. There is no penalty for incorrect answers. Each correct answer is worth one point. You will have five minutes to complete the test.

Directions: For each item, circle the letter of the correct answer.
1. Change your answer only when you are sure it is
   a. too long.
   b. too short.
   c. correct.
   d. incorrect.

2. What should you do when you decide an answer choice is incorrect?
   a. Reread the answer choice.
   b. Cross out the answer choice.
   c. Rewrite the answer choice.
   d. Guess at the answer.

3. Do not answer an item about whose answer you are unsure unless
   a. you do not understand the item.
   b. you cannot read some of the words.
   c. there is no penalty for incorrect answers.
   d. it is a hard item.

4. What should you do to key words in an item?
   a. Cross them out.
   b. Underline them.
   c. Ignore them.
   d. Rewrite them.

5. Read the _____ with each answer choice to decide which answer is correct.
   a. key words
   b. question or statement
   c. first word in an item
   d. last word in an item

Check your answers as your teacher goes over them with you. Count your number correct and use this chart to see how you did.

   5 items correct = Excellent
   4 items correct = Good
   0–3 items correct = Review the information in 10-4 and 10-5.

Here are some things you should do to help you choose the correct answer choice for a true/false item. Add information to each thing to do as your teacher discusses it with you.

- Choose **TRUE** unless you are sure that a statement is **FALSE**.

- For a statement to be **TRUE**, everything about the statement must be **TRUE**. For example, the following statement is **TRUE** because everything about it is **TRUE**.

> Maine, Ohio, and California are states that are a part of the United States.

This statement is **TRUE** because Maine, Ohio, and California are states that are a part of the United States.

Now look at this statement:

> New York, Florida, and England are states that are a part of the United States.

This statement is **FALSE** because not all parts of the statement are **TRUE**. England is a country. It is not a state that is a part of the United States.

- Be careful when a statement has a negative such as *not, do not,* or *in* (infrequent) and *un* (unfriendly). A negative can completely change the meaning of a statement. For example:

1. George Washington was the first president of the United States.

2. George Washington was not the first president of the United States.

or

1. Twelve months is a complete year.

2. Twelve months is an incomplete year.

- If a statement has two negatives, cross out both negatives. This will make it easier for you to understand the statement. For example, look at the two statements that follow. The second statement is easier to understand because the two negatives have been crossed out.

1. You will not get good grades if you do not study.

2. You will ~~not~~ get good grades if you ~~do not~~ study.

- Absolute statements are usually **FALSE**. Absolute statements include such terms as *all, every, never, no.*

  For example, this statement is **FALSE** because the word *all* makes it an absolute statement.

  > All presidents of the United States were born in Virginia.

- Qualified statements are usually **TRUE**. Qualified statements include such terms as *some, most, sometimes, rarely*

  For example, this statement is **TRUE** because the word *some* makes it a qualified statement.

  > Some presidents of the United States were born in Virginia.

- If you are not sure about an item, take a guess at the answer unless there is a penalty for guessing.

Take this sample true/false test to show what you have learned. There is no penalty for incorrect answers. Each correct answer is worth one point. You will have five minutes to complete the test.

Directions: Circle **TRUE** or **FALSE** for each of the following.

TRUE   FALSE   1. A negative can completely change the meaning of a statement.

TRUE   FALSE   2. Absolute statements are usually false.

TRUE   FALSE   3. If any part of a statement is false, then the statement is false.

TRUE   FALSE   4. If you are not certain that a statement is false, consider it false.

TRUE   FALSE   5. Qualified statements are usually false.

TRUE   FALSE   6. If a statement has two negatives, you should cross out one of the negatives.

TRUE   FALSE   7. If there is a penalty for incorrect answers, guess on any item for which you are unsure whether the statement is true or false.

Check your answers as your teacher goes over them with you. Count your number correct and use this chart to see how you did.

> 7 items correct = Excellent
> 5 or 6 items correct = Good
> 0–4 items correct = Review the information in 10-7.

Look at the matching test item. Matching test items require that you match words or terms in one column with words or terms in a second column. In the item shown, countries in the first column are matched with continents in the second column. The answers are written to show you how to do this.

Country	Continent
1. Canada	A. _2_ Europe
2. France	B. _4_ South America
3. China	C. _3_ Asia
4. Brazil	D. _1_ North America

Here are things to do when taking a matching test. Add information to each thing to do as your teacher explains it to you.

- Read all of the items in both columns before making any matches.

- Start by making the matches about which you are sure.

- Cross out items in both columns as you make matches.

- Make your best guess for remaining items unless there is a penalty for incorrect answers.

Here are two matching tests. Use what you have learned about taking matching tests as you take each test. There is no penalty for guessing. Your teacher will go over the answers with you.

Directions for Test One: Write the number for each person next to the thing for which they are famous.

1. Thomas Edison   A. ____   United States marshal in Wild West

2. Martin Luther King, Jr.   B. ____   creator of Mickey Mouse

3. Neil Armstrong   C. ____   first man to walk on the moon

4. Wyatt Earp   D. ____   African American civil rights leader

5. Walt Disney   E. ____   inventor of electric light bulb

Directions for Test Two: Write the letter for each description of a body function next to the part of the body that controls that function.

____ 1. liver   A. tissue protecting the front of the eye

____ 2. ligament   B. tissue fastening bones together at the joints

____ 3. stomach   C. bone plates that protect the brain

____ 4. cornea   D. organ in which food is digested

____ 5. cranium   E. organ that removes wastes from the blood

Each item on a completion test is a statement with part of the statement missing. The missing part of the statement can be anywhere in the statement. The missing part is shown by a line. You must write the missing part on the line to complete the statement.

Here are examples of completion test items with the missing part in different places. Answers are written to show you how they look when the item is answered.

1. When one country brings in a product that was made in another country, it is said to import that product.

2. Denver is the capital of Colorado and is its largest city.

3. The Gulf of Mexico is bordered by the southern coast of the United States and the eastern coast of Mexico.

Here are some things you should do to do well on a matching test. Add information to each thing to do as your teacher discusses it with you.

• Read the statement and think about what is missing.

• Write an answer that logically completes the statement.

• Be sure your answer fits the statement grammatically.

• Use the length of the blank line as a clue to the length of the answer unless the length of the blank line is the same for every item.

• After you write your answer on the blank line, read the entire statement to make sure your answer makes sense.

Use what you have learned about taking completion tests as you take this test. There is no penalty for guessing. Your teacher will go over the answers with you.

Directions: Complete each statement by writing the missing part on the blank line.

1. A _____ is one word that is made up of two words that have been shortened.

2. The Sphinx is an enormous stone statue built by the ancient _____ .

3. _____ is the capital of Greece.

4. Mammals are warm-blooded animals with hair that make milk to _____ their young.

5. A _____ is an instrument that uses lenses to make small, very close objects appear larger.

6. The largest ocean is the world is the _____ Ocean.

7. Waterloo is the small village in Belgium where _____ was finally defeated.

8. Coal, oil, and natural gas are fossil _____ .

9. The first ten amendments to the Constitution are called the _____ .

10. The freezing point is the _____ at which something freezes.

QUOTE is a strategy that will help you to do well when taking essay tests. Each letter in the acronym stands for one of the five steps in **QUOTE**. Write more information about each step as your teacher explains it to you.

Question is the first step. Here you ask, "What is the direction word in the test item?" A direction word tells you what you must do to answer the item. Examples of direction words are *discuss, describe, explain.*

Underline is the second step. Underline the words that help you focus on the ideas you will develop in your answer.

Organize/Write is the third step. Organize the facts and write your answer.

Time is the fourth step. Decide how much time you should spend answering each item.

Evaluate is the fifth and final step. Evaluate the content and organization of what you wrote. Also evaluate your writing mechanics.

Question is the first step you should apply in the **QUOTE** strategy for answering essay test items. Ask: "What is the direction word in the test item?" Identify and bracket [ ] the direction word. For example, look at how the direction word was bracketed in this essay test item.

> The government of the United States has three branches: executive, judicial, and legislative. [Describe] the executive branch.

Here are three direction words often used in essay test items. Read to find what each tells you to do.

Discuss tells you to give reasons behind points of view.

Describe tells you to present a detailed picture of something in words.

Explain tells you to give the reason for something.

Bracket [   ] the direction word in each of these essay test items.

1. The Revolutionary War was the war for independence fought in the late 1700s by the American colonies against England. Explain why the colonies went to war.

2. The Democratic party is one of the two main parties in American politics. Discuss the Democratic party's approach to the problem of poverty.

3. Gravity is the force that pulls objects toward each other. Briefly describe how gravity affects your life.

Here are more direction words used in essay test items. Read what each direction word tells you to do. Write more information about each direction word as your teacher tells you more about it.

List: Present information in some order.

Trace: State a series of events in logical order.

Relate: Show how two or more things are related.

Diagram: Create a visual representation to show something.

Compare: Tell how two or more things are alike and different.

Criticize: Make positive and negative comments about something.

Evaluate: Judge the merits of something using certain criteria.

Summarize: State the major points about something.

Each of these essay test items is missing a direction word. Write an appropriate direction word in the space provided.

1. _____ the major ideas of the Democratic Party and the Republican Party.

2. John F. Kennedy was a popular president of the United States. _____ his performance as president.

3. The Civil War was fought between the northern states and the southern states. _____ the events that led to this war.

4. _____ the facts you know about the life of Helen Keller.

Underline is the second step you should apply in the **QUOTE** strategy for answering essay test items. After you have bracketed [   ] the direction word, underline the words that tell you to what you must respond in the test item. Look at this example in which the direction word has been bracketed and words underlined.

> The Great Depression was the worst economic period in American history. [Explain] <u>why</u> the <u>Great Depression happened</u> when it did.

For each of these essay test items, [   ] the direction words and underline the words that tell you to what you must respond in the test item.

1. Exercise should be an important part of everyone's life. Describe how exercise can help you to lead a healthy and satisfying life.

2. Controversy still exists about whether the United States was right to fight a war in Vietnam. Trace the events that led to our involvement in the Vietnam war.

3. The Constitution of the United States is the document that established the national government of the United States. Explain what the Founding Fathers tried to accomplish when they wrote this important document.

4. Communism remains a major economic and political system in many parts of the world. Compare communist forms of government with democratic forms of government with respect to election of leaders.

5. Discuss the major positions taken by President Clinton as he campaigned to be reelected in 1996.

Organize/Write is the third step you should apply in the **QUOTE** strategy for answering an essay test item. This is what you should do for this step:

1. Look at or write the words you underlined in the essay test item.

2. Write the facts that are related to the words you underlined.

3. Organize the facts by creating a graphic organizer.

4. Using the graphic organizer as a guide, write your answer.

Here is how to write a one-paragraph answer to an essay test item:

- Begin with an introductory sentence that contains your main point.
- Follow this sentence with sentences that support your point.
- End your answer with a sentence that states your conclusion.

Here is what to do when writing an answer that has more than one paragraph:

- Begin with an introductory paragraph that contains your main point.
- Follow with additional paragraphs, each of which has supporting points.
- End with a paragraph in which you state your conclusion.

Use what you have learned in the **Organize/Write** step to write a one paragraph answer for the following essay test item.

Describe what you have learned to do on each day when using the Five-Day Test Preparation Plan.

Time is the fourth step you should apply in the **QUOTE** strategy for answering essay test items. For this step you must decide how much time you should spend answering each item on an essay test. Here is what you should do to decide how much time to spend answering each item:

- Determine the total time you have to complete the test.

- If you do not have to answer all items, decide which items you will answer.

- Consider how many points each item is worth. Plan to use more time for the items that count for the most points.

- Write in front of each item the amount of time you plan to use answering the item.

- Plan some time to review each answer.

- Make sure that the time you plan for answering and reviewing each item is not greater than the total time you have to take the test. If the time you planned is greater than the total time, revise your plan.

Pretend that you are about to take an essay test that has four items. The test counts for 100 points. You must answer all items. The first item is worth 40 points. Each of the other three items is worth 20 points. You have exactly 60 minutes to take the test.

1. What is the total time you have to take the test?

2. For which item should you use the most time?

3. Write the amount of time you plan to use for each item:

   Item 1

   Item 2

   Item 3

   Item 4

4. Add to find the total time you planned to use answering and reviewing the four items. Write that amount here.

5. Is your total planned time greater than the total time you have to take the test?

6. What should you do if your planned time is greater then the time allowed to take the test?

Evaluate is the fifth and final step you should apply in the **QUOTE** strategy for answering essay test items.

Evaluate the essay test answer you wrote in 10-17 by circling YES or NO for each of the following statements.

Content

I answered all parts of the item.	YES	NO
I included all the relevant facts.	YES	NO
All of my facts are accurate.	YES	NO

Writing

My answer begins with an introduction.	YES	NO
My answer has supporting points.	YES	NO
My answer ends with a conclusion.	YES	NO

Mechanics

My handwriting is legible.	YES	NO
I spelled all words correctly.	YES	NO
I used correct punctuation.	YES	NO
I used correct grammar.	YES	NO

What can you do to improve the answer you wrote for the essay item in 10-17?

Show what you have learned about preparing for and taking different types of tests by answering each of the following:

1. **Explain** the five things you should do to prepare for tests.

2. **List** the steps in the five-day test preparation plan.

3. **Summarize** what you should do in taking each of the following types of tests:

   Multiple-Choice

   True/False

   Matching

   Completion

4. Write what each letter in the **QUOTE** strategy reminds you to do when taking an essay test.

10-1 1. Begin to prepare early.   2. Ask the teacher what the test will cover.   3. Ask your teacher what type of test will be given.   4. Gather the information needed to study.   5. Use remembering strategies to remember the information.

10-2 Day 5. Highlight information to be remembered.

Day 4. Use remembering strategies.

Day 3. Rewrite information in brief form.

Day 2. Think of questions and write answers.

Day 1. Review rewritten notes and questions and answers.

10-3 D. Read test directions carefully and ask teacher to explain anything not known.

E. Examine test to see how much there is to do.

T. Decide how much time to spend answering each item.

E. Answer easiest questions first.

R. Review answers.

10-4 Responses will vary but should conform to the formats shown for the two types.

10-5 Notes will vary.

10-6 1. d.   2. b.   3. c.   4. b.   5. b.

10-7 Notes will vary.

10-8 1. True.   2. True.   3. True.   4. False.   5. False.   6. False.   7. False.

10-9 Notes will vary.

10-10 Test One: A4;   B5;   C3;   D2;   E1.

Test Two: E1;   B2;   D3;   A4;   C5.

10-11 Notes will vary.

10-12 1. contraction.   2. Egyptians.   3. Athens.   4. feed.   5. microscope.   6. Pacific.   7. Napoleon.   8. fuels.   9. Bill of Rights.   10. temperature.

10-13 Notes will vary.

10-14 1. Explain.   2. Discuss.   3. Describe.

10-15 Responses may vary. Suggested responses are: 1. Compare.   2. Evaluate or criticize.   3. Trace.   4. List or summarize.

10-16 Suggested answers follow:

1. Exercise should be an important part of everyone's life. [Describe] how exercise can help you to lead a healthy and satisfying life.

2. Controversy still exists about whether the United States was right to fight a war in Vietnam. [Trace] the events that led to our involvement in the Vietnam war.

3. The Constitution of the United States is the document that established the national government of the United States. [Explain] what the Founding Fathers tried to accomplish when they wrote this important document.

4. Communism remains a major economic and political system in many parts of the world. [Compare] communist forms of government with democratic forms of government with respect to election of leaders.

5. [Discuss] the major positions taken by President Clinton as he campaigned to be re-elected in 1996.

10-17 Responses will vary but should contain the information presented in 10-2. Here is an example of an appropriate response:

A five-day test preparation plan helps you get ready for a test and get a high score on the test. You need to begin studying five days before the test. On the fifth day before a test, get all the information you need to know. On the fourth day, use remembering strategies to remember the information. On the third day, rewrite the information in the fewest words. On the second day before the test, think of questions that your teachers might ask and write answers for each. On the day of the test, review one last time. The five-day test preparation strategy will make you prepared for your test and improve your grades.

10-18 1. 60 minutes. 2. First item. 3. Responses may vary. Sample responses are: Item 1, 20 minutes; Item 2, 15 minutes; Item 3, 15 minutes; Item 4, 10 minutes. 4. Responses will vary. 5. Responses will vary. 6. Revise your planned use of time.

10-19 Responses will vary.

10-20 1. Same as for 10-1. 2. Same as for 10-2. 3. Multiple-choice: Guidelines shown on 10-5; True/false: Guidelines shown on 10-7; Matching: Guidelines shown on 10-9; Completion: Guidelines shown on 10-11. 4. Q = Question, U = Underline, O = Organize/write, T = Time, E = Evaluate.

Making Good Use of Study Time and Space

OBJECTIVES

1. Teach students a strategy for making good use of study time.
2. Teach students to assess and improve their study habits.
3. Teach students to assess and improve their study place.

TITLES OF REPRODUCIBLE ACTIVITIES

11-1 A Strategy for Making Good Use of Study Time
11-2 Learning about a Term Calendar
11-3 Term Calendar
11-4 Learning about a Weekly Planner
11-5 Weekly Planner
11-6 Learning about a Daily Planner
11-7 Daily Planner
11-8 Checking My Study Habits
11-9 Improving My Study Habits
11-10 Checking My Study Place
11-11 Improving My Study Place
11-12 Chapter Eleven Mastery Assessment
Answer Key

USING THE REPRODUCIBLE ACTIVITIES

11-1 A Strategy for Making Good Use of Study Time

Lead students in a discussion of the importance of using time effectively. Tell them that successful students schedule and manage their time to complete their schoolwork and responsibilities, yet still have some time for fun. Explain each of the three steps in the strategy for making good use of study time. Have students write statements about what should be done in each step.

11-2 Learning about a Term Calendar
11-3 Term Calendar

Discuss the purposes of a term calendar. Review the three things students should do to use a term calendar. Have students list on 11-2 their school assignments, school activities, and out-of-school activities for the term. Tell students to include dates. Distribute copies of 11-3. Have students record information from 11-2 on 11-3.

11-4 Learning about a Weekly Planner
11-5 Weekly Planner

Discuss the purposes of a weekly planner. Review the three things students should do to prepare a weekly planner. Have students complete the lists in 11-4 for the coming week. Distribute copies of 11-5. Have students record information from 11-4 on 11-5. Repeat this procedure for each week.

11-6 Learning about a Daily Planner
11-7 Daily Planner

Discuss the purposes of a daily planner. Review the five things students do to prepare a daily planner. Have students complete the lists in 11-6 for the next day. Distribute copies of 11-7. Have students record information from 11-6 on 11-7. Remind students to complete a daily planner each evening before a school day.

11-8 Checking My Study Habits

Lead students in a discussion of the importance of good study habits. Then have students complete 11-8.

11-9 Improving My Study Habits

Have students write any study habits for which they checked "No" on 11-8. For each habit, have them write what they will do to improve it. Have students share what they will do with the class.

11-10 Checking My Study Place

Discuss with students the importance of having a good place to study. Then have students complete 11-10.

11-11 Improving My Study Place

Have students write any study place feature for which they checked "No" on 11-10. For each study place feature included, have them write what they will do to improve it. Have students share what they will do with the class.

11-12 Chapter Eleven Mastery Assessment

Have students complete this assessment at any point you feel they have learned about good use of time and space and good study habits. Review the results of the assessment with the students. Provide additional instruction as needed.

A Strategy for Making Good Use of Study Time

Have you ever felt as though you have too much schoolwork to do and not enough time to do it? You cannot do anything to change the amount of schoolwork you have. That is up to your teachers. But you can change the way in which you use the time you have.

Here is a three-step strategy you can use to make good use of your study time:

Step 1   Prepare a **term calendar**. This calendar should show all your important school and out-of-school activities and assignments for a term. Prepare a term calendar at the beginning of each school term. Add new items to your calendar as the term goes on.

Step 2   Prepare a **weekly planner**. This planner should show your school and out-of-school activities and assignments for a week. Prepare a weekly planner at the beginning of each school week. Add new items as the week goes on.

Step 3   Prepare a **daily planner**. This planner should show what you must do each day and when you plan to do it. Prepare a daily planner each night for the next school day.

Write a statement that tells what you must do for each step in the strategy for making good use of your study time.

1.

2.

3.

To do all the things you want to do each term, you need to schedule your time. A term calendar will remind you when you need to start and finish important school and out-of-school activities. It will help you plan your time so you can get done everything you must do.

A term calendar helps you to organize your school and out-of-school activities for an entire term. Here is how you use a term calendar:

1. Ask each of your teachers for a list of assignments and due dates. Write them on your term calendar.

2. Get a list of the school activities for the current term and their dates. Write them on your term calendar.

3. Make a list of the out-of-school activities in which you plan to be involved. These include such things as attending sporting events, going to club meetings, and going on family trips. Write the activities and dates on your term calendar.

   Now list the school assignments you know you will have this term. Also write the dates.

   Then list the school activities you know you will be involved with this term. Also write the dates.

   Next list the out-of-school activities you know you will be involved with this term. Also write the dates.

   Finally, use these lists to complete the term calendar provided by your teacher.

Name: _____

Dates Covered: _____

Monday	Tuesday	Wednesday	Thursday	Friday

Use a weekly planner to show in detail what you are planning to do during a school week. Here is how to prepare a weekly planner:

Each Sunday evening:

1. Review your term calendar to see what you planned to do during the upcoming week. Enter this information into your weekly planner.

2. Review notes from your classes to see what else needs to be added to your weekly planner.

3. Think of the out-of-school activities you need to add to your weekly planner.

Now list items from your term calendar that you need to record on your weekly planner.

Then list items from your class notes you nee to record on your weekly planner.

Next, list out-of-school activities you need to record on your weekly planner.

Finally, use these lists to complete the weekly planner provided to you by your teacher.

Weekly Planner

NAME _____   WEEK OF _____

	MONDAY	TUESDAY	WEDNESDAY	THURSDAY	FRIDAY	SATURDAY	SUNDAY
9:00							
10:00							
11:00							
12:00							
1:00							
2:00							
3:00							
4:00							
5:00							
EVENING							

Each evening before a school day, you should prepare a daily planner. The daily planner shows how you will use your time that day. Here is how to prepare a daily planner.

1. Review your weekly planner to see what you need to do tomorrow.

2. Review your class notes to see what you need to do tomorrow.

3. Review your daily planner for today to determine what you did not get done. Add these things to your daily planner for tomorrow.

4. For each thing you need to do tomorrow, decide how much time you need to do it.

5. Decide when you will do each thing. Write the thing you need to do in the appropriate time period in your daily planner.

Now list the things from your weekly planner that you need to do tomorrow. Next to each, tell how much time you need to do it.

Then list things from your class notes you know you need to do tomorrow. Next to each, tell how much time you need to do each thing.

Next, list things you did not finish from today's daily planner that you will need to do tomorrow. Next to each, tell how much time you need to do each thing.

Finally, use these lists to complete the daily planner provided by your teacher.

NAME _____   DAY/DATE _____

7:00 _____

8:00 _____

9:00 _____

10:00 _____

11:00 _____

12:00 _____

1:00 _____

2:00 _____

3:00 _____

4:00 _____

5:00 _____

6:00 _____

7:00 _____

8:00 _____

Read each study habit. If it is something you do most of the time, place a ✔ under Yes. If not, place a ✔ under No.

My Study Habits	Yes	No
I have a planned study time.		
I tell my friends not to call me during my study time.		
I start working on time.		
I review my notes before beginning an assignment.		
I begin with the hardest assignment.		
I finish one assignment before going on to another.		
I take short breaks when I feel tired.		
I avoid daydreaming.		
I have a "study buddy" I can contact when I get stuck.		
I write down questions I will need to ask my teacher.		
I keep working on long-term assignments.		

Improving My Study Habits

Write each study habit for which you checked "No" when completing 11-8. Then write a sentence that tells what you will do to improve each study habit.

Study habit to be improved:

What I will do to improve it:

Study habit to be improved:

What I will do to improve it:

Study habit to be improved:

What I will do to improve it:

Study habit to be improved:

What I will do to improve it:

Study habit to be improved:

What I will do to improve it:

Study habit to be improved:

What I will do to improve it:

Study habit to be improved:

What I will do to improve it:

Study habit to be improved:

What I will do to improve it:

Read each feature of a study place. If your study place has the feature, place a ✔ under Yes. If it does not, place a ✔ under No.

My Study Place	*Yes*	*No*
It is quiet.		
There are no things that take attention away from working.		
There is good light.		
The temperature is comfortable.		
There is a comfortable chair.		
It contains all needed work materials.		
It contains all needed reference sources.		
It contains a desk or table large enough to work at comfortably.		
It contains enough storage space.		
It can be used whenever needed.		

Write each feature for which you checked "No" when completing 11-10. Then write a sentence that tells what you will do to improve each study place feature.

Feature that needs to be improved:

What I will do to improve it:

Feature that needs to be improved:

What I will do to improve it:

Feature that needs to be improved:

What I will do to improve it:

Feature that needs to be improved:

What I will do to improve it:

Feature that needs to be improved:

What I will do to improve it:

Directions   Show what you have learned about study time, habits, and space by writing an answer for each of the following.

1. Why should you prepare a term calendar?

2. Weekly planner?

3. Daily planner?

4. How can checking your study habits help you become a better student?

5. How can checking your study place help you become a better student?

11-1 1. Prepare a term calendar showing important things to do both in- and out-of-school for the term.   2. Prepare a weekly calendar showing in- and out-of-school activities for a week.   3. Prepare a daily planner to show what must be done each day.

11-2 Responses will vary.

11-3 Entries will vary according to the information recorded on 11-2.

11-4 Responses will vary.

11-5 Entries will vary according to the information recorded on 11-4.

11-6 Responses will vary.

11-7 Entries will vary according to the information recorded on 11-6.

11-8 Responses will vary.

11-9 Entries will vary according to the information recorded on 11-8.

11-10 Responses will vary.

11-11 Entries will vary according to the information recorded on 11-10.

11-12 1. To have a long-range plan for organizing your in-school and out-of-school activities for the term.   2. To prepare for the upcoming week.   3. To show what you must do each day and when you plan to do it.   4. By identifying study habits that need to be improved. 5. By identifying study place features that need to be improved.

Bibliography

Adetumbi, M. (1992). *You're a better student than you think: A guide to memory improvement, effective study skills, and motivation for academic success.* Huntsville, AL: Adex.

Adler, B. (1988). *The student's memory book.* New York: Doubleday.

Barclay, A. (1995). *Teaching electronic information literacy: A how-to-do-it manual.* New York: Neal-Shuman.

Brescher, A., & Abamont, G. W. (1990). *Study smart! Ready-to-use reading/study skills activities for grades 5–12.* West Nyack, NY: Center for Applied Research in Education.

Bromley, K. D., & Irwin-DeVitis, L. (1995). *Graphic organizers: Visual strategies for active learning.* New York: Scholastic Professional Books.

Cherney, E. E. (1993). *Achieving academic success: A learning skills handbook,* 2nd ed. Dubuque, IA: Kendall/Hunt.

Chernow, F. B. (1986). *Ready-to-use thinking skills activities for grades 4–8.* West Nyack, NY: Parker.

Conan, M., & Heavers, K. (1994). *What you need to know about developing study skills, taking notes and tests, using dictionaries and libraries.* Lincolnwood, IL: NTC Publishing Group.

Colligan, L. (1982). *Taking tests.* New York: Scholastic Book Services.

Devine, T. G. (1987). *Teaching study skills: A guide for teachers,* 2nd ed. Boston: Allyn and Bacon.

Dodge, J. (1994). *Study skills handbook: More than 75 strategies for better learning.* New York: Scholastic.

Forgan, H. W., & Mangrum, C. T. II. (1989). *Teaching content area reading skills,* 4th ed. Columbus, OH: Merrill.

Fry, R. W. (1996). *How to study,* 4th ed. Franklin Lakes, NJ: Career Press.

Gall, M. D. (1990). *Tools for learning: A guide to teaching study skills.* Alexandria, VA: Association for Supervision and Curriculum Development.

Gayles, Y., & Deloach, A. (1996). *Every young person's guide to much better grades: A treasury of study tips, tricks, and secrets for any student who chooses success.* Chicago: Inner Working Books.

Garrett, L. J., & Moore, J. (1993). *Teaching library skills in the middle and high school: A how-to-do-it manual.* New York: Neal-Schuman.

Hoover, J. J. (1988). *Teaching handicapped students study skills*, 2nd ed. Lindale, TX: Hamilton Publications.

Hoover, J. J., & Patton, J. R. (1995). *Teaching students with learning problems to use study skills: A teacher's guide.* Austin, TX: Pro-Ed.

Krantz, H., & Kimmelman, J. (1992). *Keys to reading and study skills*, 4th ed. Fort Worth, TX: Holt, Rinehart and Winston.

Learning disabilities: Methods and materials: study skills. (1976). Videocassette. Livonia, MI: Madonna College.

Mastropieri, M. A., & Scruggs, T. E. (1987). *Effective instruction for special education.* Boston: College-Hill Press.

Mastropieri, M. A., & Scruggs, T. E. (1991). *Teaching students ways to remember: Strategies for learning mnemonically.* Cambridge, MA: Brookline Books.

McInerney, C. F. (1989). *Find it! The inside story at your library.* Minneapolis, MN: Lerner Publications.

McPherson, K. R. (1992). *Problem solving strategies (adaptable for grades 1 through 12),* 2nd ed. Killeen, TX: McPherson Problem Solving Associates.

Moody, R. B. (1995). *Coming to terms: Subject search strategies in the school library media center.* New York: Neal-Schuman.

Pavlak, S. A. (1985). *Classroom activities for correcting specific reading problems.* West Nyack, NY: Parker.

Paras, R. C. (1995). *Strategies for reading and study skills.* Lincolnwood, IL: NTC Publishing Group.

Reed, W. (1996). *Study skills the key to student success.* Dubuque, IA: Kendall/Hunt.

Robinson, H. A. (1978). *Teaching reading and study skills: The content areas,* 2nd ed. Boston: Allyn and Bacon.

Scruggs, T. E., & Mastropieri, M. A. (1992). *Teaching test-taking skills: Helping students show what they know.* Cambridge, MA: Brookline Books.

Shepherd, J. R. (1982). *The Houghton Mifflin study skills handbook.* Boston: Houghton Mifflin.

Semones, J. K. (1991). *Effective study skills: A step-by-step system for achieving student success.* Fort Worth, TX: Holt, Rinehart and Winston.

Stern, J. M. (1996). *Many ways to learn: Young people's guide to learning disabilities.* Magination Press.

Strichart, S. S., & Mangrum, C. T. II. (1993). *Teaching study strategies to students with learning disabilities.* Boston: Allyn and Bacon.

Weinstein, C. E., Goetz, E. T., & Alexander, P. A. (1988). *Learning and study strategies.* San Diego, CA: Academic Press.

Order Form

Study Skills and Strategies Assessment - Special Edition (3S-SE)

MANGRUM-STRICHART LEARNING RESOURCES

Ordering Information:

Schools: Enclose purchase order number, authorized signature and title.

Individuals: Orders must be prepaid. Please enclose check or money order.

Teachers: You may order as an individual or your school will be billed if you provide an approved purchase order number.

Quantity	Item	Price	Subtotal
_____	3S-SE disk with unlimited administrations License for use on 1 computer	$ 54.95	_____
_____	3S-SE disk with unlimited administrations License for use on 2-5 computers	$ 164.95	_____
_____	3S-SE disk with unlimited administrations License for use on 6-30 computers	$ 399.95	_____

Florida Residents add 6% Sales Tax.. _____

or include Tax Exempt Number_____

Shipping and Handling... $4.95

Check format desired: Windows_____ Macintosh_____   **TOTAL ORDER** [_____]

Method of Payment — check one

☐ Check enclosed for _____

☐ Money order enclosed for_____

☐ Bill us. Purchase order No._____
   (Schools Only -- Purchase order with authorized signature and title enclosed)

Send all orders to:

MANGRUM-STRICHART LEARNING RESOURCES
Order Department
9841 SW 122 Street
Miami, FL 33176

Please make check or money order payable to:

MANGRUM-STRICHART LEARNING RESOURCES
prices subject to change

Thank you for your order!

Ship to: *(Please print)*

Name_____

School_____

Address_____

City_____

State_____Zip_____

Telephone No. (_____)_____

Bill to: *(Please print)*

Name_____

School_____

Address_____

City_____

State_____Zip_____

Purchase Order No._____

Telephone No. (_____)_____

A companion book containing reproducible activities,**Teaching Study Skills and Strategies to Students with Learning Disabilities, Attention Deficit Disorders, or Special Needs**, is available from: Allyn and Bacon Order Department, P.O. Box 10695, Des Moines, IA 56336-0695 or call 1-800-278-3525.

LICENSING AGREEMENT

You should carefully read the following terms and conditions before opening this disk package. Opening this disk package indicates your acceptance of these terms and conditions. If you do not agree with them, you should promptly return the package unopened.

Allyn and Bacon provides this Program and License its use. You assume responsibility for the selection of the Program to achieve your intended results, and for the installation, use, and results obtained from the Program. This License extends only to use of the Program in the United States or countries in which the Program is marketed by duly authorized distributors.

License Grant

You hereby accept a nonexclusive, nontransferable, permanent License to install and use the Program on a single computer at any given time. You may copy the Program solely for backup or archival purposes in support of your use of the Program on the single computer. You may not modify, translate, disassemble, decompile, or reverse engineer the Program, in whole or in part.

Term

This License is effective until terminated. Allyn and Bacon reserves the right to terminate this License automatically if any provision of the License is violated. You may terminate the License at any time. To terminate this License, you must return the Program, including documentation, along with a written warranty stating that all copies of the Program in your possession have been returned or destroyed.

Limited Warranty

The Program is provided "As Is" without warranty of any kind, either express or implied, including, but not limited to, the implied warranties or merchantability and fitness for a particular purpose. The entire risk as to the quality and performance of the Program is with you. Should the Program prove defective, you (and not Allyn and Bacon or any authorized distributor) assume the entire cost of all necessary servicing, repair, or correction. No oral or written information or advice given by Allyn and Bacon, its dealers, distributors, or agents shall create a warranty or increase the scope of its warranty.

Some states do not allow the exclusion of implied warranty, so the above exclusion may not apply to you. This warranty gives you specific legal rights and you may also have other rights that vary from state to state.

Allyn and Bacon does not warrant that the functions contained in the Program will meet your requirements or that the operation of the Program will be uninterrupted or error free.

However, Allyn and Bacon warrants the disk(s) on which the Program is furnished to be free from defects in material and workmanship under normal use for a period of ninety (90) days form the date of delivery to you as evidenced by a copy of your receipt.

The Program should not be relied on as the sole basis to solve a problem whose incorrect solution could result in injury to a person or property. If the Program is employed in such a manner, it is at the user's own risk and Allyn and Bacon explicitly disclaims all liability for such misuse.

Limitation of Remedies

Allyn and Bacon's entire liability and your exclusive remedy shall be:

1. The replacement of any disk not meeting Allyn and Bacon's "Limited Warranty" and that is returned to Allyn and Bacon or

2. If Allyn and Bacon is unable to deliver a replacement disk or cassette that is free of defects in materials or workmanship, you may terminate this Agreement by returning the Program.

In no event will Allyn and Bacon be liable to you for any damages, including any lost profits, lost savings, or other incidental or consequential damages arising out of the use or inability to use such Program even if Allyn and Bacon or an authorized distributor has been advised of the possibility of such damages of for any claim by any other party.

Some states do not allow the limitation or exclusion of liability for incidental or consequential damages, so the above limitation or exclusion may not apply to you.

General

You may not sublicense, assign, or transfer the License of the Program. Any attempt to sublicense, assign, or transfer any of the rights, duties, or obligations hereunder is void.

This Agreement will be governed by the laws of the State of Massachusetts.

Should you have any questions concerning this Agreement, or any questions concerning technical support, you may contact Allyn and Bacon by writing to:

Allyn and Bacon
Simon and Schuster Education Group
160 Gould Street
Needham Heights, MA 02194

You acknowledge that you have read this Agreement, understand it, and agree to be bound by its terms and conditions. You further agree that it is the complete and exclusive statement of the Agreement between us that supersedes any proposal or prior Agreement, oral or written, and any other communications between us relating to the subject matter of this Agreement.

Notice to Government End Users

The Program is provided with restricted rights. Use, duplication, or disclosure by the Government is subject to restrictions set forth in subdivison (b)(3)(iii) of The Rights in Technical Data and Computer Software Clause 252.227-7013.